Explore the Science of Positivity, Growth and Resilience

POWER of POSITIVE MINDSET

Transform Attitude, Embrace Growth Mindset, Build Resilience and Master Your Mind in 30 Days

By

Samapti Banerjee

Copyright © 2024 by Samapti Banerjee

All rights reserved. No part of this book may be reproduced in any form without permission in writing from the author.

No part of this publication may be reproduced or transmitted in any form or by any means, mechanical or electronic, including photocopying or recording, by any information storage and retrieval system, or by email or any other means whatsoever without permission in writing from the author.

Objective Of The Book

10 key objectives of the book "Power of Mindset":

Understanding the basic concept and importance of mindset: Clearly realize the concept of mindset and differentiate between fixed and growth mindsets.

Explore benefits: Explore the benefits of adopting a positive and growth-oriented mindset in personal and professional contexts.

Promote resilience: Discuss how embracing a growth mindset enhances resilience, adaptability, and perseverance.

Overcome self-limiting beliefs: Provide practical strategies to identify and overcome self-limiting beliefs that hinder personal growth.

Offer practical tools: Equip readers with actionable techniques and exercises to cultivate a growth mindset in their daily lives.

Share real-life examples: Illustrate the transformative power of mindset through real-life stories and research findings.

Encourage continuous learning: Emphasize the importance of lifelong learning and continuous development in sustaining a growth mindset.

Create supportive environments: Offer tips for creating environments and communities that foster growth-oriented mindsets.

Empower personal growth: Guide readers in setting and achieving personal and professional goals through mindset shifts.

Inspire action: Inspire readers to take proactive steps towards achieving their aspirations by leveraging the power of mindset.

These objectives collectively aim to empower readers with the knowledge and tools necessary to embrace a growth mindset and unlock their full potential in all aspects of life.

Unlock Your Gift Bundles

Grab your FREE PDF Blueprint

As you have grabbed my book and reached this stage, I believe you are curious to develop good intentions and to learn more. As a token of appreciation, I would like to offer you this gift.

Visit https://winning-thinker-8854.ck.page/92cd3161e1 and get my Book FREE. It will be delivered to your email inbox.

Over 130 pages book in pdf comprising 11 chapters.

Understand psychology behind incremental growth, need for celebrating small victories, understand power of mindset, and foster letting go through small wins.

How To Use The Book

Follow the guidelines as stated below on how to effectively use the book "Power of Mindset" to maximize its benefits:

1. Start with Intention:

Begin by setting clear intentions for reading the book. Reflect on what you hope to achieve—whether it's overcoming self-limiting beliefs, enhancing resilience, or achieving personal growth.

2. Dive into Each Chapter:

Read each chapter attentively, focusing on understanding the key concepts presented. Take notes on important insights, practical strategies, and exercises provided.

3. Reflect and Apply:

After reading each section, take time to reflect on how the concepts resonate with your own experiences and challenges. Consider how you can apply the strategies discussed to cultivate a growth-oriented mindset in your daily life.

4. Engage with Exercises:

Participate actively in the exercises and activities suggested throughout the book. These are designed to help you practice and internalize the principles of mindset transformation.

5. Track Progress:

Keep a journal or notebook to track your progress and reflections as you implement new mindset practices. Note any changes in your thinking patterns, behaviors, or responses to challenges.

6. Discuss and Share:

Engage in discussions with friends, colleagues, or a book club about the concepts and strategies from the book. Sharing insights and learning from others' perspectives can deepen your understanding and motivation.

7. Review and Reinforce:

Periodically revisit chapters or sections that resonate most with you. Use these reviews as opportunities to reinforce positive habits and refresh your commitment to mindset growth.

8. Set Goals and Take Action:

Based on what you've learned, set specific goals aligned with your aspirations. Use the book's guidance to take actionable steps towards achieving these goals, leveraging your newfound mindset tools.

9. Embrace Lifelong Learning:

Understand that adopting a growth mindset is a journey, not a destination. Continuously seek opportunities to learn and grow, applying the principles from the book in new situations and challenges.

10. Share Your Successes:

Celebrate your successes along the way, no matter how small. Share your achievements with others to inspire and encourage them on their own journeys of mindset development.

By following these steps, you can effectively utilize "Power of Mindset" as a practical guide to transform your mindset, achieve personal growth, and unlock new possibilities in your life.

DEDICATION

This book is dedicated to all those seeking to fulfill their aspirations to live a meaningful and prosperous life.

Acknowledgment

I would like to acknowledge the support received from various people and organizations with whom I was associated for considerable time and who have contributed a lot to develop my knowledge base, starting from school and service life; whose collective wisdom has illuminated the path toward empowered thinking.

I would prefer first to express my deep heartfelt gratitude to my grandparents and great grandparents who have always desired us to learn continuously and share wisdom with others.

I am grateful to my spouse, my child, other senior family members, relatives and teachers for their support and for giving me the inspiration, courage and total support to continue learning and sharing lessons.

I thank my sisters for supporting me always to write books to share my thoughts to help the aspiring adults across the globe.

I am grateful to the eminent authors with whom I interact, whose books I read and learn a lot, whose videos I watch and gain lot of knowledge to share with others. I am grateful to them from the core of my heart for being inspired to share my thoughts to help people to solve their problems.

I am grateful to be inspired by Google scholar, various websites, ChatGPT, TEDx Talks, YouTube and such other sites for enriching my knowledge base.

I am thankful to the readers and audiences for showing interest in my articles, books and educational videos. Their feedback and enthusiasm have motivated me to continue exploring the profound concepts of intentional thinking and attraction.

Welcome

Dear Reader,

Welcome to "Power of Positive Mindset" by Samapti Banerjee. I am delighted to embark on this transformative journey with you—a journey that explores the profound impact of mindset on our lives and the limitless possibilities it unlocks.

In these pages, you will discover the power of your thoughts to shape your reality. Whether you are seeking personal growth, professional success, or simply a more fulfilling life, understanding and cultivating a growth-oriented mindset will be your guiding light.

Together, we will explore the concepts of resilience, adaptability, and perseverance—qualities that empower us to navigate life's challenges with grace and determination. Through real-life examples, practical strategies, and insights grounded in research, "Power of Mindset" will equip you with the tools to overcome self-limiting beliefs and embrace a mindset of growth and possibility.

I invite you to open your mind and heart to the transformative power of mindset. Let this book be your companion as you embark on a journey of self-discovery, empowerment, and achievement. May it inspire you to unleash your full potential and lead a life filled with purpose and resilience.

Thank you for joining me on this enriching adventure. Together, let's embrace the power of mindset and unlock a future brimming with endless opportunities.

Warm regards,

Samapti Banerjee

Preface

As I reflect on my own journey and the countless heavenly experiences that have shaped my path, one theme stands out prominently: the power of mindset. It is with great enthusiasm and a sense of purpose that I present to you "Power of Mindset". This book is born out of my deep-seated belief in the transformative potential of our thoughts and attitudes.

My interest in this topic stems from personal encounters with challenges and triumphs, where I witnessed firsthand how fixing one's mindset on any endeavor can profoundly impact outcomes. Whether navigating career transitions, overcoming setbacks, or pursuing personal goals, I have seen how embracing a growth-oriented mindset can turn obstacles into steppingstones for success.

Through "Power of Mindset", my intention is clear: to empower you, the reader, with practical insights and strategies to cultivate a resilient and growth-oriented mindset. This book is not just about theory; it is a roadmap filled with actionable steps to help you break free from self-limiting beliefs, embrace challenges with confidence, and sustain long-term personal and professional growth.

By sharing real-life examples, backed by research and practical exercises, I aim to provide you with the tools necessary to harness the full potential of your mindset. Whether you are embarking on a new career, seeking personal fulfillment, or striving for greater resilience in the face of adversity, "Power of Mindset" is designed to be your companion and guide.

I invite you to embark on this journey with me. Together, let us explore the profound impact of mindset on our lives and unlock the boundless possibilities that await us.

Let us jointly explore further why mindset matters:

Understanding the power of mindset goes beyond mere positivity; it shapes our responses to challenges and influences our ability to adapt and thrive in an ever-changing world. "Power of Positive Mindset" explores how shifting our mindset can lead to profound personal and professional growth, offering a framework to transform setbacks into opportunities for learning and advancement.

A personal commitment:

Writing this book has been a deeply personal journey for me, driven by a commitment to share insights that have enriched my own life. I believe in the potential of every individual to cultivate a mindset that fosters resilience, innovation, and continuous improvement. My hope is that through these pages, you will discover new perspectives and practical strategies that empower you to achieve your aspirations with clarity and confidence.

Looking ahead:

As you embark on the chapters ahead, consider this not just as a book to read, but as a toolkit to apply in your daily life. Each concept, exercise, and example are crafted to provoke thought and inspire action. Whether you are just beginning to explore the power of mindset or seeking to deepen your understanding, I invite you to engage wholeheartedly and embrace the journey of growth and discovery that "Power of Mindset" offers.

Table Of Contents

Introduction 25
Story 25

Cultivating a Growth Mindset 28

Chapter 1: Understanding Mindset 33

1.1 Elevated mindset and importance of cultivating a growth-oriented mindset 33

1.2 Explore the origins of mindset theory and its implications for individual development 41

1.3 Provide examples and anecdotes illustrating the influence of mindset on various aspects of life 53

Summary of Chapter 1: Understanding Mindset 57

Key Takeaways 59

Action Steps 61

Chapter 2: The Power of Growth Mindset 65

2.1 Explore deep into the characteristics and benefits of a growth-oriented mindset 67

2.2 Discuss how embracing a growth mindset leads to increased resilience, adaptability, and motivation 70

2.3 Share research findings and real-life examples demonstrating the transformative power of adopting a growth mindset 82

Summary of Chapter 2: "The Power of Growth Mindset" 89

Key Takeaways 91

Action Steps 92

Chapter 3: Overcoming Self-Limiting Beliefs 97

3.1 Identify common self-limiting beliefs that hinder personal growth and success 101

3.2 Offer practical strategies and exercises for challenging and reframing negative thoughts and beliefs..105

3.3 Provide guidance on building self-awareness and cultivating a positive, empowering mindset..113

Summary of Chapter 3: Overcoming Self-Limiting Beliefs...................120

Key Takeaways 121

Action Steps...123

Chapter 4: Cultivating a Growth Mindset 127

4.1 Explore techniques for fostering a growth-oriented mindset in oneself and others 129

4.2 Discuss the role of effort, persistence, and learning from failure in developing a growth mindset..133

4.3 Offer tips for creating environments and communities that support and encourage growth and development................................137

Summary for Chapter 4: Cultivating a Growth Mindset......................140

Key Takeaways 142

Action Steps...144

Chapter 5: Embracing Challenges and Failures 151

5.1 Examine the relationship between mindset and resilience in the face of challenges and setbacks 153

5.2 Share stories of individuals who have turned adversity into opportunity through a growth-oriented mindset..................................158

5.3 Provide strategies for reframing failure as a learning experience and fuel for growth...161

Summary of Chapter 5: Embracing Challenges and Failures 168

Key Takeaways 170

Action Steps...171

Chapter 6: Nurturing Growth in Others 175

6.1 Discuss the importance of fostering a growth mindset in children, students, employees, and team members...178

6.2 Offer practical techniques for providing constructive feedback, praise, and encouragement that promote a growth-oriented mindset .181

6.3 Highlight the role of leadership in creating environments that foster continuous learning and development. 185

Summary of Chapter 6: Nurturing Growth in Others............................190

Key Takeaways 192

Action Steps..194

Chapter 7: Sustaining Growth and Momentum 199

7.1 Explore strategies for maintaining a growth mindset over the long term...204

7.2 Discuss the importance of self-care, goal-setting, and ongoing learning in sustaining personal growth and resilience.........................213

7.3 Provide guidance on overcoming obstacles and staying motivated on the journey to realizing one's full potential 218

Summary of Chapter 7: Sustaining Growth and Momentum...............224

Key Takeaways 226

Action Steps 229

Conclusion 233

Outcome of the Book 245

Scope for Further Research 251

May I Request You for a Review? 255

Disclaimer 257

Appendices 259

References for Further Learning 289

About the Author 295

More Books From the Author 297

The Upcoming Book 299

Introduction

Story

In the vast expanse of ancient India, amidst the kingdom of Hastinapur, a pivotal moment in history unfolded—a tale of honor, duty, and the profound impact of mindset. It was an era when kingdoms clashed, alliances were tested, and destinies were shaped by the choices of individuals who dared to challenge the status quo.

At the heart of this epic saga, the Mahabharata, lies the story of Arjuna, a skilled warrior and prince of the Pandavas dynasty. As tensions escalated towards an inevitable war, Arjuna found himself standing on the battlefield of Kurukshetra, surrounded by friends, foes, and the weight of his own uncertainties.

On that fateful day, as the war horns echoed and the clamor of chariots filled the air, Arjuna faced a moment of profound introspection. He gazed upon his opponents—his own kin, revered teachers, and beloved friends assembled on both sides of the battlefield. Overwhelmed by doubt and moral quandary, Arjuna turned to his charioteer, Lord Krishna, seeking guidance in the midst of this moral crisis.

What unfolded next was not just a dialogue between a warrior and his charioteer, but a discourse on the very essence of mindset—a discourse that would resonate through the ages. Lord Krishna imparted to Arjuna the wisdom of dharma (righteous duty), urging him to rise above attachment and fear, to embrace his role as a warrior with clarity and resolve.

In this moment, Arjuna's mindset underwent a transformation. He moved from doubt to determination, from confusion to clarity, and from hesitation to action. With a newfound perspective, he took up his bow, the Gandiva, and prepared to fulfill his destiny with unwavering conviction.

The story of Arjuna on the battlefield of Kurukshetra serves as a timeless reminder of the power of mindset. It illustrates how our beliefs, attitudes, and perceptions can shape our decisions and actions, influencing not only our personal journeys but also the course of history itself. Just as Arjuna's mindset played a pivotal role in the Mahabharata, so too can our mindset determine the outcomes of our own battles—whether they be internal struggles or external challenges we face in our modern lives.

As we embark on this exploration of mindset in "Power of Mindset," let us draw inspiration from Arjuna's journey. Let us reflect on how our mindset influences our choices, shapes our ambitions, and ultimately defines our path to fulfillment and success.

The concept of mindset and its profound impact on attitudes, behaviors, and outcomes.

Mindset refers to the established beliefs, attitudes, and assumptions that shape how individuals perceive and interpret the world around them, ultimately influencing their attitudes, behaviors, and outcomes. This concept, popularized by psychologist Carol Dweck, highlights the profound impact of our mindset on various aspects of life.

Understanding Mindset Types:

Fixed Mindset: In a fixed mindset, individuals believe that abilities, intelligence, and talents are innate and unchangeable. They may avoid challenges for fear of failure, feel threatened by the success of others, and view setbacks as indicators of personal limitations.

Growth Mindset: Conversely, a growth mindset involves the belief that abilities and qualities can be developed through dedication, effort, and learning. People with a growth mindset embrace challenges, persist in the face of setbacks, and see failures as opportunities for growth and improvement.

Impact on Attitudes:

Resilience: A growth mindset fosters resilience by encouraging individuals to see challenges as learning opportunities rather than insurmountable obstacles. This resilience enables them to bounce back from setbacks more effectively.

Optimism: Those with a growth mindset tend to maintain a positive outlook, believing in their ability to improve and achieve goals through effort and perseverance.

Impact on Behaviors:

Effort and Persistence: Individuals with a growth mindset are more likely to exert effort and persist in pursuing goals, even when faced with difficulties or setbacks.

Learning and Adaptation: They actively seek opportunities to learn and develop new skills, continually adapting to changes and challenges in their environment.

Impact on Outcomes:

Achievement and Success: Research indicates that individuals with a growth mindset are more likely to achieve higher levels of success in academics, careers, sports, and personal endeavors. They approach tasks with a belief that their efforts can lead to improvement and mastery over time.

Innovation and Creativity: A growth mindset promotes innovation and creativity by encouraging individuals to explore new ideas, take calculated risks, and challenge conventional thinking.

Cultivating a Growth Mindset

Self-Awareness: Recognize and challenge fixed mindset thoughts and beliefs. Cultivate awareness of how your mindset influences your thoughts, behaviors, and responses to challenges.

Embrace Challenges: Approach challenges as opportunities for growth and learning rather than threats to your self-esteem or competence.

Learn from Feedback: Value constructive feedback as a means to learn and improve. Use feedback to adjust strategies and refine skills.

Encourage Others: Foster a growth mindset in others by providing encouragement, support, and constructive feedback. Create an environment that values effort, perseverance, and continuous learning.

Mindset plays a pivotal role in shaping our attitudes, behaviors, and outcomes in life. By cultivating a growth mindset, individuals can enhance their resilience, achieve greater success, and foster a more optimistic and adaptable approach to challenges and opportunities.

Let us differentiate between a fixed mindset and a growth mindset using examples to illustrate their contrasting beliefs and behaviors:

Example 1: Approach to Challenges

Fixed Mindset:

Belief: "I'm either good at something or I'm not. If I struggle with it, it means I'm just not talented in that area."

Behavior: A student with a fixed mindset might avoid taking advanced courses or participating in challenging projects because they fear failure or looking incompetent. They stick to what they know they can do well to protect their self-image.

Growth Mindset:

Belief: "Challenges are opportunities to learn and improve. With effort and perseverance, I can develop my skills."

Behavior: A student with a growth mindset actively seeks out challenges. They enroll in difficult courses or take on projects that stretch their abilities because they believe in their capacity to learn and grow through effort. Even if they initially struggle, they see setbacks as temporary and learn from them to improve.

Example 2: Response to Setbacks

Fixed Mindset:

Belief: "If I fail at something, it means I'm just not cut out for it."

Behavior: An employee with a fixed mindset may become discouraged and disengaged after receiving negative feedback or encountering a setback at work. They might avoid similar tasks in the future to avoid risking failure again.

Growth Mindset:

Belief: "Setbacks are a natural part of learning and growth. They provide valuable feedback that helps me improve."

Behavior: An employee with a growth mindset sees setbacks as opportunities for reflection and improvement. They actively seek feedback from colleagues and supervisors, use setbacks as learning experiences, and adjust their approach to achieve better results in the future.

Example 3: Effort and Persistence

Fixed Mindset:

Belief: "If I have to work hard at something, it means I'm not naturally talented."

Behavior: A musician with a fixed mindset might give up practicing a difficult piece of music if they don't master it quickly. They may believe that struggling indicates a lack of innate ability and that further effort will not make a difference.

Growth Mindset:

Belief: "Effort and persistence are the keys to mastery. The more I practice, the better I will become."

Behavior: A musician with a growth mindset embraces the process of learning and improvement. They practice consistently, seek guidance from mentors, and are willing to invest the time and effort needed to refine their skills. They understand that mastery is achieved through dedication and continuous learning.

In each example, the differences between a fixed mindset and a growth mindset are evident in their beliefs about abilities, responses to challenges and setbacks, and attitudes towards effort and persistence. A fixed mindset tends to limit individuals by viewing abilities as static and avoiding challenges or setbacks that could threaten their self-image. In contrast, a growth mindset promotes resilience, embraces challenges as opportunities for growth, and believes in the power of effort and learning to achieve success. Cultivating a growth mindset can lead to greater personal fulfillment, resilience, and achievement in both personal and professional endeavors.

Chapter 1: Understanding Mindset

"Whether you think you can, or you think you can't – you're right."

– Henry Ford

1.1 Elevated mindset and importance of cultivating a growth-oriented mindset

Mindset transcends mere belief systems; it embodies a dynamic framework that shapes our perception, resilience, and ability to harness potential. At its core, mindset represents the culmination of our beliefs, experiences, and deliberate choices, influencing how we interpret challenges, embrace growth, and cultivate resilience in pursuit of our aspirations.

Key Elements of an Elevated Mindset:

Conscious Awareness and Intentionality:

An elevated mindset begins with conscious awareness of our thoughts and beliefs. It involves intentional cultivation of positive, adaptive beliefs that empower us to navigate complexities with clarity and purpose.

Emotional Intelligence and Adaptability:

Beyond resilience, an elevated mindset emphasizes emotional intelligence and adaptability. It encourages the recognition and regulation of emotions, fostering a balanced perspective that fuels constructive actions and enriches interpersonal dynamics.

Inclusive Growth and Collaboration:

Elevating mindset transcends individual achievement to embrace inclusive growth and collaboration. It champions the collective elevation of perspectives and contributions, catalyzing innovation and sustainable progress.

Transformative Leadership and Impact:

At its zenith, mindset inspires transformative leadership and impact. It champions visionary leadership rooted in empathy, humility, and ethical stewardship, driving systemic change and advancing societal well-being.

Impact on Attitude:

An elevated mindset profoundly influences attitude, serving as a cornerstone for cultivating positivity, resilience, and purpose-driven actions:

Positive Resilience: It fosters a resilient attitude that views setbacks as opportunities for growth and refinement, rather than impediments to progress.

Optimistic Outlook: Embracing an elevated mindset nurtures an optimistic outlook that energizes creativity, innovation, and solution-oriented thinking amidst challenges.

Empathetic Engagement: It promotes empathetic engagement, nurturing relationships grounded in mutual respect, trust, and collaboration.

Practical Application:

Reflective Practice: Engage in reflective practices that foster self-awareness and alignment with values, facilitating intentional mindset cultivation.

Continuous Learning: Embrace a growth-oriented approach to learning and development, continuously expanding perspectives and capabilities.

Purposeful Action: Translate mindset into purposeful action, fostering environments conducive to personal and collective flourishing.

In essence, an elevated concept of mindset transcends conventional boundaries, embodying a transformative force that empowers individuals and communities to navigate complexities with resilience, compassion, and visionary leadership. By embracing and embodying this elevated mindset, individuals can catalyze positive change, inspire others, and collectively shape a future rooted in shared prosperity and well-being.

Cultivating a growth-oriented mindset is crucial for achieving personal and professional success.

Here are several key reasons why this mindset is essential:

1. Continuous Learning and Adaptation:

A growth-oriented mindset emphasizes the importance of continuous learning and development.

It encourages individuals to seek out new knowledge, skills, and experiences, fostering adaptability in an ever-changing world.

2. Resilience in the Face of Challenges:

Individuals with a growth mindset view challenges and setbacks as opportunities for growth and learning, rather than as failures.

This resilience enables them to bounce back stronger, persevere through obstacles, and maintain motivation in pursuit of their goals.

3. Innovation and Creativity:

Embracing a growth mindset fosters creativity and innovation by encouraging individuals to explore new ideas and approaches.

It promotes a willingness to take risks, experiment with different solutions, and think outside the box to solve problems effectively.

4. Enhanced Problem-Solving Abilities:

People with a growth mindset are better equipped to tackle complex problems and find solutions.

They approach challenges with a positive attitude, leveraging their skills and knowledge to overcome obstacles and achieve desired outcomes.

5. Career Advancement and Professional Development:

In professional settings, a growth-oriented mindset is highly valued by employers and leaders.

It signals an employee's willingness to learn, adapt to change, and take on new responsibilities, which can lead to career advancement and opportunities for leadership roles.

6. Positive Attitude and Mental Well-Being:

Adopting a growth mindset promotes a positive attitude towards oneself and others.

It reduces stress, anxiety, and self-doubt by reframing setbacks as learning experiences and fostering a sense of optimism about one's abilities and potential.

7. Building Strong Relationships & Collaboration:

Individuals with a growth mindset are open to feedback, willing to learn from others, and supportive of collaborative efforts.

They build strong relationships based on trust, respect, and mutual support, which enhances teamwork and collective achievement.

8. Achieving Personal Fulfillment and Satisfaction:

Cultivating a growth-oriented mindset empowers individuals to pursue meaningful goals and aspirations.

It increases satisfaction and fulfillment in life by aligning actions with personal values, passions, and aspirations.

9. Contributing to Continuous Improvement:

A growth mindset contributes to a culture of continuous improvement within organizations and communities.

It inspires others to embrace change, innovate, and strive for excellence in their respective fields.

In essence, cultivating a growth-oriented mindset is instrumental in unlocking personal and professional success. It enables individuals to embrace challenges, foster creativity, build resilience, and continuously learn and adapt to achieve their full potential and make meaningful contributions to their communities and beyond.

The consequences of NOT cultivating a growth-oriented mindset

Not cultivating a growth-oriented mindset can have significant consequences for both personal and professional success.

Here are some key consequences:

1. Stagnation and Lack of Progress:

Without a growth-oriented mindset, individuals may become complacent and resistant to change.

They may avoid challenges and opportunities for learning, leading to stagnation in skills and knowledge.

2. Limited Resilience and Adaptability:

A fixed mindset can hinder resilience in the face of setbacks and failures.

Individuals may struggle to bounce back from challenges, viewing setbacks as permanent and indicative of personal shortcomings.

3. Fear of Failure and Risk Aversion:

Those with a fixed mindset often fear failure and avoid taking risks that could lead to growth and innovation.

This fear of failure can prevent individuals from seizing new opportunities and exploring their full potential.

4. Diminished Learning and Development:

Without a growth mindset, individuals may miss out on valuable learning experiences and opportunities for personal development.

They may resist feedback and constructive criticism, hindering their ability to improve and grow professionally.

5. Negative Impact on Relationships and Collaboration:

Fixed mindset attitudes can lead to interpersonal challenges, such as difficulty in accepting others' perspectives and reluctance to collaborate.

This can hinder teamwork, innovation, and collective problem-solving efforts.

6. Limitations in Goal Achievement:

A fixed mindset may limit individuals' ability to set ambitious goals and persist in their pursuit.

They may settle for mediocrity rather than striving for excellence and continuous improvement.

7. Impact on Career Advancement:

In professional settings, a fixed mindset can hinder career advancement and opportunities for promotion.

Employers value employees who demonstrate a growth mindset, as they are more likely to innovate, adapt to change, and contribute positively to organizational goals.

8. Missed Opportunities for Innovation and Creativity:

A growth-oriented mindset fosters creativity and innovation by encouraging individuals to explore new ideas and approaches.

Without this mindset, individuals may miss opportunities to innovate and contribute to meaningful change in their industries or fields.

9. Overall Decrease in Satisfaction and Fulfillment:

Ultimately, a fixed mindset can lead to decreased job satisfaction and overall fulfillment in life.

Individuals may feel stuck in their careers or personal lives, lacking the motivation and resilience needed to pursue meaningful goals and aspirations.

In summary, not cultivating a growth-oriented mindset can limit personal and professional success by hindering resilience, stifling innovation, and impeding learning and development. Embracing a growth mindset, on the other hand, empowers individuals to embrace challenges, learn from setbacks, and continuously evolve to achieve their full potential.

1.2 Explore the origins of mindset theory and its implications for individual development

The concept of mindset was popularized by psychologist Carol Dweck in her groundbreaking research on achievement and success, particularly in the context of education. Dweck's theory originated from her observations and experiments aimed at understanding why some students thrive and excel while others struggle, even when faced with similar challenges and opportunities.

Origins of Mindset Theory:

Early Research and Observations:

Carol Dweck began her research in the 1970s, exploring children's attitudes and responses to failure.

She noticed that some students rebounded from setbacks with renewed determination, while others seemed devastated and demoralized by even minor failures.

Fixed vs. Growth Mindset Distinction:

Through extensive studies and experiments, Dweck identified two distinct mindsets that individuals adopt: fixed mindset and growth mindset.

Fixed Mindset: Believing that abilities and intelligence are static traits, leading to a desire to prove oneself and avoid failure.

Growth Mindset: Believing that abilities can be developed through effort and learning, leading to a desire for learning and resilience in the face of challenges.

Implications for Individual Development:

Learning and Achievement: Individuals with a growth mindset tend to embrace challenges and view setbacks as opportunities for learning and improvement. This attitude fosters a love for learning and resilience in the face of obstacles, contributing to academic and professional success.

Resilience and Adaptability: Adopting a growth mindset encourages individuals to persist through difficulties and setbacks. They are more likely to seek constructive feedback, learn from criticism, and adjust their strategies accordingly, which enhances their ability to adapt to changing circumstances.

Motivation and Effort: A growth mindset promotes intrinsic motivation by emphasizing the role of effort and persistence in achieving goals. It shifts the focus from proving oneself to continually improving, fostering a sense of agency and control over one's success.

Emotional Well-being: Cultivating a growth mindset can enhance emotional well-being by reducing fear of failure and increasing self-compassion. Individuals are less likely to perceive setbacks as reflections of their innate abilities, which mitigate stress and anxiety.

Social and Interpersonal Relationships: In educational and professional settings, promoting a growth mindset can create a supportive environment where individuals collaborate, share ideas, and support each other's development. It fosters a culture of learning and continuous improvement.

Practical Applications:

Education: Mindset theory has significant implications for teaching and learning. Educators can cultivate a growth mindset in students by praising effort and perseverance rather than solely focusing on intelligence or talent. This approach encourages students to embrace challenges and develop resilience.

Leadership and Management: In organizational settings, leaders can foster a growth mindset culture by promoting learning and development, providing opportunities for skill-building, and encouraging innovation and risk-taking.

Personal Development: Individuals can apply mindset theory to their own lives by reflecting on their beliefs about abilities and effort. By cultivating a growth mindset, they can set ambitious goals, persist through challenges, and achieve personal and professional growth.

In conclusion, mindset theory has revolutionized our understanding of human potential and development by emphasizing the role of beliefs in shaping attitudes, behaviors, and outcomes. By promoting a growth mindset, individuals and organizations can unlock untapped potential, foster resilience, and cultivate a culture of continuous learning and improvement.

Varied concepts of other renowned researchers and writers on mindset

In addition to Carol Dweck's pioneering work on mindset, several other renowned researchers and writers have contributed complementary concepts and perspectives that enrich our understanding of mindset and its implications for personal and professional development. Here are some key concepts from other influential figures:

1. Angela Duckworth - Grit

Concept: Angela Duckworth introduced the concept of "grit," which she defines as passion and perseverance for long-term goals.

Key Points: Grit involves sustaining effort and interest over years despite setbacks, adversity, and plateaus in progress.

Implications: Duckworth's research suggests that grit is a crucial factor in achieving high levels of success and accomplishment, often more so than talent alone.

2. Anders Ericsson - Deliberate Practice

Concept: Anders Ericsson's research focuses on "deliberate practice," which refers to purposeful and focused practice aimed at improving specific aspects of performance.

Key Points: Deliberate practice involves breaking down skills into components, setting specific goals for improvement, and receiving feedback to refine performance.

Implications: Ericsson's work highlights the role of deliberate effort and practice in developing expertise and achieving mastery in various domains.

3. Martin Seligman - Positive Psychology

Concept: Martin Seligman is known for his work in positive psychology, which emphasizes strengths, virtues, and factors that contribute to human flourishing.

Key Points: Positive psychology explores topics such as happiness, well-being, resilience, optimism, and the cultivation of positive emotions.

Implications: Seligman's approach encourages individuals to focus on building strengths, fostering positive emotions, and enhancing overall life satisfaction and fulfillment.

4. Daniel Kahneman - Dual Process Theory

Concept: Daniel Kahneman's dual process theory distinguishes between two systems of thinking: System 1 (fast, intuitive, and automatic) and System 2 (slow, deliberate, and analytical).

Key Points: System 1 operates automatically and quickly, while System 2 involves more effortful and deliberate reasoning.

Implications: Understanding these cognitive processes helps individuals recognize biases, make better decisions, and become more aware of how their thinking influences their behaviors and outcomes.

5. Steven Covey - Paradigm Shifts

Concept: Steven Covey introduced the concept of "paradigm shifts," which involves a fundamental change in perspective or worldview.

Key Points: Covey emphasizes the importance of shifting from a reactive mindset (being driven by circumstances) to a proactive mindset (taking responsibility for one's choices and actions).

Implications: Paradigm shifts enable individuals to adopt a more empowered and proactive approach to personal and professional challenges, leading to greater effectiveness and success.

6. Malcolm Gladwell - 10,000-Hour Rule

Concept: Malcolm Gladwell popularized the "10,000-hour rule," which suggests that achieving mastery in any field requires approximately 10,000 hours of deliberate practice.

Key Points: Gladwell's concept underscores the importance of sustained effort and practice over time in developing expertise and achieving exceptional performance.

Implications: While the exact number of hours may vary, the principle highlights the significance of dedication, persistence, and focused practice in skill development and mastery.

7. Ellen Langer - Mindfulness

Concept: Ellen Langer's work on mindfulness challenges traditional notions of mindlessness and encourages active engagement and awareness in everyday activities.

Key Points: Mindfulness involves being fully present in the moment, noticing new things, and questioning assumptions to foster creativity and personal growth.

Implications: Practicing mindfulness can enhance cognitive flexibility, improve decision-making, and promote well-being by reducing stress and increasing resilience.

8. Shawn Achor - Positive Intelligence

Concept: Shawn Achor focuses on the concept of "positive intelligence," which involves developing positive habits of mind that lead to greater happiness and success.

Key Points: Achor emphasizes the power of positive thinking, gratitude, and optimism in improving performance, resilience, and overall well-being.

Implications: Cultivating positive intelligence through daily practices can enhance productivity, creativity, and interpersonal relationships, contributing to sustained personal and professional success.

These concepts from renowned researchers and writers provide diverse perspectives on mindset, skill development, resilience, positivity, and cognitive processes. Each contributes valuable insights into how individuals can enhance their capabilities, achieve goals, and lead more fulfilling lives by adopting proactive, growth-oriented approaches to personal and professional development. Integrating these concepts can empower individuals to navigate challenges, capitalize on strengths, and continually strive for excellence in their chosen endeavors.

How these mindset theories effect on individual development

Mindset theories, including those from Carol Dweck, Angela Duckworth, Anders Ericsson, Martin Seligman, Daniel Kahneman, Steven Covey, Malcolm Gladwell, Ellen Langer, and Shawn Achor, have profound effects on individual development across various aspects of life. Here's how these theories influence and contribute to individual growth and development:

1. Adopting a Growth Mindset (Carol Dweck):

Impact: Individuals who embrace a growth mindset believe that abilities and intelligence can be developed through dedication and hard work.

Effect on Development: This mindset fosters a love for learning, resilience in the face of challenges, and a belief in the power of effort. It encourages individuals to seek out opportunities for growth, persist through setbacks, and continuously improve their skills and knowledge.

2. Cultivating Grit (Angela Duckworth):

Impact: Grit involves passion and perseverance towards long-term goals, even in the face of adversity and setbacks.

Effect on Development: Developing grit helps individuals sustain effort over time, maintain focus on achieving goals, and navigate obstacles with determination. It promotes resilience, self-discipline, and the ability to overcome challenges to achieve meaningful success.

3. Deliberate Practice (Anders Ericsson):

Impact: Deliberate practice focuses on purposeful and focused efforts to improve specific skills or abilities.

Effect on Development: By engaging in deliberate practice, individuals can systematically enhance their performance, acquire expertise, and achieve mastery in their chosen fields.

This approach emphasizes the importance of focused effort, feedback, and continuous refinement of skills.

4. Positive Psychology (Martin Seligman):

Impact: Positive psychology emphasizes strengths, well-being, and factors that contribute to human flourishing.

Effect on Development: Integrating principles of positive psychology into one's life promotes resilience, optimism, and a focus on personal strengths and virtues. It enhances overall life satisfaction, mental well-being, and the ability to cope with challenges effectively.

5. Dual Process Theory (Daniel Kahneman):

Impact: Kahneman's theory distinguishes between intuitive, automatic thinking (System 1) and deliberate, analytical thinking (System 2).

Effect on Development: Understanding dual process theory helps individuals become aware of cognitive biases, improve decision-making processes, and approach problems with a more balanced and informed perspective. It promotes critical thinking, effective problem-solving, and better judgment.

6. Paradigm Shifts (Steven Covey):

Impact: Covey's concept encourages individuals to shift from a reactive to a proactive mindset, taking responsibility for their choices and actions.

Effect on Development: Embracing paradigm shifts enables individuals to adopt a more empowered and proactive approach to personal and professional challenges. It fosters personal growth, leadership development, and the ability to influence positive change in oneself and others.

7. 10,000-Hour Rule (Malcolm Gladwell):

Impact: Gladwell's rule suggests that achieving mastery in any field requires approximately 10,000 hours of deliberate practice.

Effect on Development: While the exact number of hours may vary, the principle underscores the importance of sustained effort, persistence, and dedication in skill development. It motivates individuals to commit to continuous learning, hone their expertise, and strive for excellence in their pursuits.

8. Mindfulness (Ellen Langer):

Impact: Langer's work on mindfulness promotes active engagement, curiosity, and open-mindedness in daily activities.

Effect on Development: Practicing mindfulness enhances self-awareness, reduces stress, and improves cognitive flexibility. It cultivates a deeper appreciation for the present moment, supports emotional regulation, and fosters creativity and personal growth.

9. Positive Intelligence (Shawn Achor):

Impact: Positive intelligence focuses on developing positive habits of mind that enhance happiness, resilience, and success.

Effect on Development: By fostering a positive mindset, individuals can boost their productivity, build stronger relationships, and maintain a sense of optimism in challenging situations. It promotes a proactive approach to problem-solving, fosters creativity, and enhances overall well-being.

Overall Effect on Individual Development:

Holistic Growth: Integrating these mindset theories promotes holistic development by addressing cognitive, emotional, and behavioral aspects of individuals.

Resilience and Adaptability: These theories equip individuals with the resilience to overcome setbacks, adapt to change, and navigate complex challenges effectively.

Continuous Improvement: They encourage a mindset of continuous improvement, lifelong learning, and personal growth.

Achievement of Goals: By fostering determination, focus, and a positive outlook, mindset theories empower individuals to achieve their goals and maximize their potential in various domains of life.

In summary, mindset theories profoundly influence individual development by shaping attitudes, behaviors, and outcomes. They provide frameworks and strategies that empower individuals to cultivate resilience, pursue excellence, and lead fulfilling lives characterized by continuous growth and personal achievement.

1.3 Provide examples and anecdotes illustrating the influence of mindset on various aspects of life

Examples and anecdotes illustrating the influence of mindset on various aspects of life, drawing from different mindset theories:

1. Academic Achievement and Growth Mindset

Example: Sarah's Journey to Improved Grades

Background: Sarah used to believe she wasn't good at math. She often avoided challenging problems and felt discouraged when she didn't understand concepts immediately.

Mindset Shift: After learning about growth mindset, Sarah started viewing math as a skill she could develop with effort.

Impact: She began practicing regularly, seeking help from teachers, and embracing mistakes as learning opportunities.

Outcome: Over time, Sarah's grades improved significantly. She went from barely passing to excelling in math, demonstrating that her belief in growth and persistence paid off.

2. Entrepreneurial Success and Grit

Example: Jack's Startup Journey

Background: Jack launched a tech startup but faced numerous setbacks and failures early on.

Mindset Shift: Inspired by Angela Duckworth's concept of grit, Jack committed himself to persisting through challenges and setbacks.

Impact: Instead of giving up when investors rejected his ideas or when the product faced technical issues, Jack refined his approach, sought feedback, and iterated on his product.

Outcome: After several iterations and with unwavering determination, Jack's startup gained traction. He secured funding, expanded his team, and eventually achieved success in the competitive tech industry.

3. Professional Development & Deliberate Practice

Example: Maya's Path to Mastery

Background: Maya, a graphic designer, wanted to enhance her illustration skills but felt stuck at an intermediate level.

Mindset Shift: Following Anders Ericsson's concept of deliberate practice, Maya set specific goals to improve her illustration techniques.

Impact: She identified areas for improvement, studied under experienced artists, and dedicated focused time each day to practice.

Outcome: Over months of deliberate practice, Maya's skills noticeably advanced. She developed a unique style, gained recognition for her work, and expanded her client base, illustrating how deliberate effort can lead to mastery in creative fields.

4. Personal Well-being and Positive Psychology

Example: David's Journey to Emotional Resilience

Background: David faced significant setbacks in his personal life, leading to feelings of despair and hopelessness.

Mindset Shift: Learning about positive psychology from Martin Seligman, David decided to focus on cultivating gratitude and optimism.

Impact: He started journaling daily about things he was grateful for, practiced mindfulness to manage stress, and reframed negative thoughts into positive ones.

Outcome: Gradually, David noticed improvements in his emotional well-being. He became more resilient, coping effectively with challenges, and fostering stronger relationships based on positivity and gratitude.

5. Leadership and Paradigm Shifts

Example: Sarah's Transformation as a Leader

Background: Sarah, a manager in a fast-paced organization, struggled with team morale and productivity issues.

Mindset Shift: Inspired by Steven Covey's concept of paradigm shifts, Sarah realized she needed to shift from a reactive to a proactive leadership style.

Impact: She started prioritizing communication, actively listening to her team's concerns, and empowering them to take ownership of their work.

Outcome: Sarah's team became more engaged, collaborative, and innovative.

They achieved higher productivity and morale, demonstrating how a proactive mindset can transform leadership and organizational culture.

6. Health and Mindfulness

Example: John's Journey to Stress Management

Background: John experienced chronic stress due to demanding work and personal responsibilities.

Mindset Shift: Learning about Ellen Langer's mindfulness principles, John decided to integrate mindfulness practices into his daily routine.

Impact: He started practicing meditation, became more aware of his thoughts and emotions, and focused on being present in each moment.

Outcome: John experienced reduced stress levels, improved sleep quality, and enhanced overall well-being. His mindful approach helped him manage challenges more effectively and maintain a balanced lifestyle.

These examples illustrate how mindset theories such as growth mindset, grit, deliberate practice, positive psychology, paradigm shifts, and mindfulness can profoundly influence various aspects of life. By adopting proactive, growth-oriented mindsets and applying relevant principles, individuals can enhance their abilities, achieve goals, navigate challenges, and ultimately lead more fulfilling and successful lives. Mindset plays a pivotal role in shaping attitudes, behaviors, and outcomes, highlighting its importance in personal development, professional success, and overall well-being.

Summary of Chapter 1: Understanding Mindset

1.1 Elevated mindset and importance of cultivating a growth-oriented mindset.

In this section, the concept of elevated mindset is introduced as the collection of beliefs, attitudes, and assumptions that shape how individuals perceive and respond to the world around them.

Two primary mindsets are explored:

Fixed Mindset: Believes abilities and intelligence are innate and unchangeable. Individuals with a fixed mindset tend to avoid challenges, fear failure, and see effort as fruitless if they lack immediate success.

Growth Mindset: Believes abilities and intelligence can be developed through dedication, effort, and learning. Those with a growth mindset embrace challenges, persist in the face of setbacks, and see effort as a path to mastery.

An elaborate explanation is shared how a growth mindset can help in personal growth.

1.2 Explore the Origins of Mindset Theory and Its Implications for Individual Development

This section explores the origins of mindset theory, notably Carol Dweck's pioneering research:

Origins: Carol Dweck's research in the 1970s examined children's responses to failure and their beliefs about intelligence. She identified fixed and growth mindsets as fundamental to how individuals approach learning and achievement.

Implications: Mindset theory has profound implications for personal and professional development. It suggests that adopting a growth mindset can enhance resilience, foster a love for learning, and empower individuals to overcome obstacles and achieve higher levels of success.

1.3 Provide Examples and Anecdotes Illustrating the Influence of Mindset on Various Aspects of Life

This section highlights real-life examples and anecdotes demonstrating the impact of mindset on different domains:

Academic Achievement: Sarah's transformation from struggling in math to excelling through adopting a growth mindset.

Entrepreneurial Success: Jack's perseverance and resilience in building a successful startup, influenced by concepts of grit and growth mindset.

Professional Development: Maya's journey to mastery in illustration by applying principles of deliberate practice and growth mindset.

Personal Well-being: David's improvement in emotional resilience and happiness through positive psychology and mindset shifts.

Leadership and Organizational Culture: Sarah's leadership transformation, leading to improved team dynamics and productivity by embracing proactive mindset strategies.

Health and Wellness: John's stress management and improved well-being through mindfulness practices rooted in mindset principles.

Chapter 1 establishes a foundational understanding of mindset, distinguishing between fixed and growth mindsets and exploring their origins and implications for personal and professional growth. Through compelling examples and anecdotes, the chapter illustrates how mindset influences academic achievement, entrepreneurial success, professional development, personal well-being, leadership, and health. It sets the stage for deeper exploration into mindset theories and practical applications in subsequent chapters.

Key Takeaways

Mindset Defined: Mindset refers to the beliefs and attitudes that shape how individuals perceive their abilities and approach challenges.

Fixed Mindset vs. Growth Mindset: Understanding the distinction between a fixed mindset (belief in innate, unchangeable abilities) and a growth mindset (belief in the ability to develop through effort and learning) is crucial for personal development.

Origins of Mindset Theory: Carol Dweck's research in the 1970s laid the foundation for mindset theory, exploring its impact on learning and achievement.

Implications for Development: Adopting a growth mindset enhances resilience, fosters a love for learning, and empowers individuals to overcome obstacles.

Academic Achievement: Individuals with a growth mindset are more likely to embrace challenges, persist through setbacks, and achieve higher levels of academic success.

Entrepreneurial Success: Grit and perseverance, influenced by mindset theory, play a critical role in entrepreneurial endeavors, helping individuals navigate challenges and achieve success.

Professional Growth: Mindset impacts professional development by influencing attitudes towards skill development, feedback, and career progression.

Personal Well-being: Positive psychology principles, rooted in mindset theory, promote emotional resilience, happiness, and overall well-being.

Leadership and Organizational Culture: Leadership effectiveness is enhanced when leaders adopt a growth mindset, fostering a culture of innovation, learning, and collaboration.

Health and Wellness: Mindfulness practices, informed by mindset principles, contribute to stress management, improved mental health, and enhanced quality of life.

These takeaways highlight the broad applicability of mindset theory across various domains of life, underscoring its transformative potential for personal growth, professional success, and well-being. Understanding and applying these principles can empower individuals to cultivate resilience, achieve goals, and lead fulfilling lives.

Action Steps

1. Embrace a Growth Mindset:

Action Step: Reflect on your beliefs about abilities and intelligence. Identify areas where you might hold a fixed mindset. Challenge these beliefs by affirming that abilities can be developed through dedication and effort.

2. Learn About Mindset Theory:

Action Step: Dive deeper into mindset theory by reading Carol Dweck's book "Mindset: The New Psychology of Success" or exploring reputable articles and resources online. Gain a thorough understanding of the differences between fixed and growth mindsets.

3. Apply Mindset Principles to Challenges:

Action Step: When faced with a challenge or setback, consciously adopt a growth mindset approach. Instead of feeling defeated, view the challenge as an opportunity to learn and grow. Emphasize the importance of effort and persistence in overcoming obstacles.

4. Foster a Learning Environment:

Action Step: Whether in an educational or professional setting, encourage a culture that values effort, learning, and resilience. Provide constructive feedback that focuses on improvement rather than innate abilities.

5. Set Growth-Oriented Goals:

Action Step: Set specific, challenging goals that align with your long-term aspirations. Break down these goals into manageable steps and commit to continuous improvement through deliberate practice and learning.

6. Cultivate Grit and Perseverance:

Action Step: Develop grit by practicing perseverance and resilience in the face of setbacks. Keep a journal to track your progress, setbacks, and lessons learned. Celebrate small wins and stay focused on long-term objectives.

7. Prioritize Personal Well-being:

Action Step: Incorporate principles of positive psychology into your daily routine. Practice gratitude by journaling about things you are thankful for. Engage in mindfulness exercises to reduce stress and enhance emotional resilience.

8. Lead with a Growth Mindset:

Action Step: If in a leadership role, model a growth mindset for your team. Encourage open communication, innovation, and learning from failures. Provide opportunities for professional development and growth.

9. Seek Feedback and Learn from Criticism:

Action Step: Approach feedback as valuable input for growth. Actively seek constructive feedback from mentors, peers, or supervisors. Use feedback to identify areas for improvement and adjust your approach accordingly.

10. Practice Mindfulness and Self-Reflection:

Action Step: Dedicate time to practice mindfulness meditation or other mindfulness techniques regularly. Use self-reflection to assess your mindset in different situations and identify opportunities for personal growth and development.

By taking these action steps, you can actively cultivate a growth mindset, enhance resilience, achieve goals more effectively, and contribute positively to your personal and professional development journey. Mindset is not just a theory but a practical framework for continuous improvement and achieving greater success in all aspects of life.

"The journey from a fixed mindset to a growth mindset is the path to unlocking our true potential and transforming our reality." – Author

In Chapter 1, we explore the intricate network of mindset, highlighting its profound impact on personal and professional growth. We explored how cultivating a growth-oriented mindset is not just advantageous but essential for navigating life's challenges and seizing opportunities. By understanding the origins of mindset theory and its evolution, we laid the groundwork for appreciating how our beliefs shape our reality. Through compelling examples and anecdotes, we witnessed firsthand the transformative influence of mindset on everything from academic achievement to career success and personal relationships.

Now, in Chapter 2, we go deeper into the transformative power of a growth mindset. We unravel the core characteristics that distinguish a growth-oriented mindset, emphasizing its role in fostering resilience, adaptability, and unwavering motivation. By examining both research findings and real-life examples, we illustrate how individuals can harness the full potential of a growth mindset to overcome setbacks and thrive in dynamic environments. This chapter serves as a beacon of inspiration, showing that embracing a growth mindset not only enhances personal development but also cultivates a mindset that fuels continuous learning and achievement.

CHAPTER 2: THE POWER OF GROWTH MINDSET

"It's not that I'm so smart, it's just that I stay with problems longer."

- Albert Einstein

In today's rapidly changing world, the concept of a growth mindset has gained significant attention. Coined by psychologist Carol Dweck, a growth mindset is the belief that abilities and intelligence can be developed through dedication and hard work. This contrasts with a fixed mindset, where individuals believe their talents are innate and unchangeable. Embracing a growth mindset can lead to remarkable achievements in personal and professional realms by fostering resilience, encouraging learning, and promoting adaptability.

A growth mindset cultivates resilience, enabling individuals to face challenges with a positive attitude. People who adopt this perspective view setbacks as opportunities to learn rather than as failures. For example, students with a growth mindset are more likely to persist through difficult coursework, understanding that struggle is a part of the learning process. This resilience not only helps in academic settings but also in personal life, where overcoming obstacles is essential for growth and development. The belief in the ability to improve empowers individuals to take risks and pursue their goals without the fear of failure holding them back.

Moreover, a growth mindset encourages a continuous pursuit of knowledge and self-improvement. Those who believe their abilities can grow are more inclined to seek out new experiences, embrace challenges, and learn from their mistakes. This attitude is particularly beneficial in professional settings, where staying updated with the latest skills and knowledge is crucial. Employees with a growth mindset are more likely to take on new projects and responsibilities, contributing to innovation and progress within their organizations. Their commitment to learning often inspires colleagues and creates a dynamic and forward-thinking workplace culture.

Adaptability is another key advantage of a growth mindset. In a world where technology and industries are constantly evolving, the ability to adapt is critical. Individuals with a growth mindset are more flexible and open to change, viewing it as an opportunity for growth rather than a threat. This adaptability not only helps in coping with changes but also in anticipating future trends and preparing for them. For instance, in the fast-paced tech industry, professionals who continuously learn and adapt are better positioned to lead and succeed. Their willingness to evolve with changing circumstances ensures long-term success and relevance.

Furthermore, adopting a growth mindset can improve relationships and collaboration. When people believe in development and growth, they are more likely to value feedback and view it as a tool for improvement rather than criticism. This perspective fosters a supportive environment where constructive feedback is encouraged, and individuals work together towards mutual growth. In educational settings, teachers with a growth mindset can inspire their students to strive for excellence, while in the workplace, leaders can motivate their teams to achieve collective goals. By promoting a culture of growth, collaboration, and mutual support, organizations and communities can thrive.

In conclusion, a growth mindset is a powerful tool that can transform lives and drive success. By fostering resilience, encouraging lifelong learning, promoting adaptability, and enhancing relationships, this mindset empowers individuals to reach their full potential. In a constantly changing world, the ability to grow and adapt is invaluable. Embracing a growth mindset not only leads to personal and professional achievements but also contributes to a culture of continuous improvement and innovation.

2.1 Explore deep into the characteristics and benefits of a growth-oriented mindset

Characteristics of a Growth-Oriented Mindset

Belief in Development: At the core of a growth-oriented mindset is the belief that abilities and intelligence can be developed through effort, learning, and persistence. People with this mindset understand that innate talent is just a starting point and that their true potential is cultivated through dedication and hard work.

Embrace of Challenges: Individuals with a growth mindset view challenges as opportunities to grow rather than obstacles to avoid. They are willing to step out of their comfort zones, take on difficult tasks, and push their limits. This attitude helps them to continuously expand their capabilities and improve their skills.

Persistence in the Face of Setbacks: Resilience is a hallmark of a growth-oriented mindset. When faced with setbacks, these individuals do not give up easily. Instead, they see failure as a part of the learning process and an opportunity to refine their strategies and approaches. They persist, understanding that perseverance is key to achieving long-term success.

Focus on Learning and Improvement: A growth mindset is characterized by a strong desire to learn and improve. These individuals are curious and open to new experiences. They seek out feedback, view it as constructive, and use it to make necessary adjustments and improvements. Their focus is on the process of learning rather than on immediate results.

Effort Over Talent: People with a growth-oriented mindset prioritize effort over innate talent. They believe that hard work, dedication, and continuous practice are more important than natural ability. This perspective motivates them to put in the necessary effort to achieve their goals and to view effort as a pathway to mastery.

Benefits of a Growth-Oriented Mindset

Enhanced Resilience: A growth mindset significantly enhances resilience. By viewing challenges and failures as opportunities to learn, individuals become more resilient and better equipped to handle adversity. This resilience is crucial for personal growth, as it allows individuals to bounce back from setbacks and continue striving towards their goals.

Increased Motivation and Engagement: The belief that abilities can be developed leads to higher levels of motivation and engagement. Individuals with a growth mindset are more likely to be intrinsically motivated, finding joy in the process of learning and improvement. This intrinsic motivation drives them to engage deeply with their tasks and to persist even when faced with difficulties.

Improved Performance: Over time, a growth-oriented mindset leads to improved performance. By consistently embracing challenges, seeking feedback, and putting in the effort, individuals enhance their skills and knowledge. This continuous improvement results in better performance in various areas, whether in academics, professional settings, or personal endeavors.

Greater Adaptability: In a world that is constantly changing, adaptability is a valuable trait. A growth mindset fosters adaptability by encouraging individuals to be open to new experiences, learn from diverse situations, and adjust their strategies as needed. This adaptability is particularly beneficial in professional environments, where staying relevant and competitive requires continuous learning and evolution.

Enhanced Relationships and Collaboration: A growth-oriented mindset also positively impacts relationships and collaboration. Individuals who believe in growth are more likely to value feedback and support the development of others. This creates a positive and supportive environment where collaboration thrives. In educational and workplace settings, this mindset fosters teamwork, mutual respect, and collective progress.

A growth-oriented mindset is a powerful attribute that offers numerous benefits. It is characterized by a belief in the potential for development, an embrace of challenges, resilience in the face of setbacks, a focus on learning, and a prioritization of effort over talent. The benefits of adopting this mindset include enhanced resilience, increased motivation and engagement, improved performance, greater adaptability, and enhanced relationships and collaboration. In an ever-changing world, cultivating a growth-oriented mindset is essential for personal and professional success. It empowers individuals to continuously learn, grow, and achieve their full potential.

"Believe in your infinite potential. Your only limitations are those you set upon yourself." – Roy T. Bennett

2.2 Discuss how embracing a growth mindset leads to increased resilience, adaptability, and motivation

Embracing a Growth Mindset: Pathways to Increased Resilience, Adaptability, and Motivation

Increased Resilience

Embracing a growth mindset fundamentally transforms how individuals perceive and respond to challenges, leading to heightened resilience. A growth mindset fosters the belief that abilities and intelligence can be developed through effort and perseverance. This belief instills a proactive approach to challenges, viewing them as opportunities for learning rather than insurmountable obstacles. When setbacks occur, individuals with a growth mindset are less likely to be discouraged because they see failure as a temporary and necessary part of the learning process. Instead of giving up, they analyze their mistakes, learn from them, and try again with improved strategies. This persistent effort and positive outlook on setbacks enhance their resilience, enabling them to bounce back stronger from adversity and continue progressing towards their goals.

Enhanced Adaptability

Adaptability is another significant benefit of a growth mindset. In a world characterized by rapid technological advancements and shifting paradigms, the ability to adapt is crucial for sustained success. A growth mindset encourages openness to new experiences and a willingness to learn from diverse situations. Individuals with this mindset do not fear change; instead, they welcome it as a chance to grow and improve. This attitude makes them more flexible in adjusting to new environments, roles, or challenges. For instance, in the workplace, an employee with a growth mindset is more likely to embrace new technologies, adopt innovative practices, and take on new responsibilities. Their adaptability not only helps them stay relevant and competitive but also positions them as valuable assets in dynamic and evolving settings. By continuously seeking growth and improvement, they can navigate changes with confidence and agility.

Heightened Motivation

A growth mindset intrinsically boosts motivation by shifting the focus from proving one's abilities to improving them. Individuals who believe in the potential for growth are more likely to be intrinsically motivated, driven by the desire to learn and achieve mastery rather than by external rewards or recognition. This intrinsic motivation fuels their passion and commitment to their goals. They are more engaged in their tasks, putting in the necessary effort and time to overcome challenges and achieve excellence. This engagement is often self-sustaining; the more they learn and improve, the more motivated they become to continue the process. Additionally, a growth mindset fosters a sense of ownership and responsibility for one's development, further enhancing motivation. People with this mindset are proactive in seeking feedback, setting goals, and pursuing opportunities for growth, leading to sustained and consistent efforts towards their aspirations.

Synergy of Resilience, Adaptability, and Motivation

The interplay between resilience, adaptability, and motivation creates a powerful synergy that propels individuals towards continuous improvement and success.

Resilience allows them to recover from setbacks and persist in the face of difficulties. Adaptability enables them to navigate and thrive in changing environments. Motivation drives them to engage deeply with their goals and maintain a persistent effort. Together, these qualities create a robust framework for personal and professional growth. For example, in an academic setting, a student with a growth mindset may encounter a challenging subject but driven by their motivation to learn, they persist despite initial failures (resilience) and adjust their study strategies (adaptability). Over time, their consistent effort and willingness to adapt lead to mastery of the subject, showcasing the transformative power of a growth mindset.

Embracing a growth mindset leads to increased resilience, adaptability, and motivation, which are essential qualities for achieving success in today's fast-paced and ever-changing world. By viewing challenges as opportunities for growth, individuals develop the resilience to overcome setbacks, the adaptability to thrive in new and evolving environments, and the intrinsic motivation to pursue continuous improvement. The synergy of these qualities fosters a proactive and persistent approach to personal and professional development, enabling individuals to reach their full potential and achieve lasting success. Adopting a growth mindset is not just about enhancing specific skills or achieving short-term goals; it is about cultivating a lifelong commitment to learning, growth, and self-improvement.

The Role of a Growth Mindset in Increasing Resilience

A growth mindset plays a crucial role in increasing resilience by shaping how individuals perceive challenges and setbacks. Here are a few points illustrating this relationship, along with examples:

1. Viewing Failures as Learning Opportunities

People with a growth mindset see failures and setbacks as valuable learning experiences rather than as reflections of their abilities. This perspective reduces the fear of failure and encourages a proactive approach to overcoming obstacles.

Example: A student who receives a low grade on a test with a growth mindset might analyze their mistakes, seek help from a teacher, and develop a better study plan for future exams. Instead of being discouraged by the poor grade, they use it as a steppingstone to improve their understanding and performance.

2. Emphasizing Effort Over Talent

A growth mindset emphasizes the importance of effort, practice, and persistence over innate talent. This belief helps individuals remain motivated and committed to their goals, even when progress is slow or difficult.

Example: An athlete who initially struggles with a new technique but believes that consistent practice will lead to improvement will persist despite early failures. Over time, their dedication to refining their skills results in mastery of the technique, demonstrating resilience in the face of initial difficulties.

3. Maintaining a Positive Outlook

A growth mindset fosters a positive outlook on challenges, viewing them as opportunities for growth rather than threats. This optimism helps individuals stay motivated and focused, even when faced with significant obstacles.

Example: An entrepreneur whose startup faces financial difficulties might see this challenge as an opportunity to learn more about financial management, explore alternative funding options, and refine their business model. Their positive attitude and willingness to adapt contribute to their resilience, enabling them to navigate and overcome the crisis.

4. Encouraging Problem-Solving and Innovation

With a growth mindset, individuals are more likely to approach problems creatively and seek innovative solutions. This problem-solving attitude enhances their ability to adapt and persist in the face of challenges.

Example: A software developer encountering a complex bug might experiment with different debugging techniques, seek input from colleagues, and research new methods. Their willingness to explore various solutions and learn from each attempt increases their resilience, ultimately leading to a successful resolution of the issue.

5. Building Self-Efficacy and Confidence

A growth mindset helps build self-efficacy, the belief in one's ability to succeed through effort and learning. This confidence in their capabilities strengthens resilience, as individuals are more likely to take on challenges and persist through difficulties.

Example: A novice public speaker who believes they can improve with practice may start with small presentations, gradually increasing the audience size and complexity of topics. Each successful experience boosts their confidence, reinforcing their belief in their ability to improve, which in turn enhances their resilience in facing future public speaking engagements.

A growth mindset significantly contributes to increasing resilience by promoting a positive and proactive approach to challenges, emphasizing effort and learning, and fostering problem-solving and innovation. By viewing failures as opportunities, maintaining a positive outlook, and building self-efficacy, individuals with a growth mindset are better equipped to navigate and overcome setbacks, leading to personal and professional growth.

The Impact of a Growth Mindset on Adaptability

A growth mindset significantly enhances adaptability by fostering a flexible, open, and proactive approach to change. Here are several ways in which a growth mindset impacts adaptability, along with examples:

1. Embracing Change as an Opportunity

Individuals with a growth mindset view change as a chance to learn and grow rather than as a threat. This positive outlook makes them more receptive to new ideas, environments, and situations.

Example: An employee in a company that is undergoing a major restructuring may see the changes as an opportunity to develop new skills, take on new roles, and contribute to the organization in different ways. This perspective allows them to adapt quickly and effectively to the new organizational structure.

2. Continuous Learning and Improvement

A growth mindset encourages a commitment to lifelong learning. Individuals are always seeking ways to improve and expand their knowledge and skills, which is essential for adapting to new circumstances.

Example: A teacher who adopts new educational technologies to enhance their teaching methods demonstrates adaptability. By continuously learning about and integrating new tools into their classroom, they can better meet the diverse needs of their students and stay current with educational trends.

3. Flexibility in Problem-Solving

People with a growth mindset are more willing to experiment with different approaches and strategies. They are not fixed on a single way of doing things and are open to trying new methods when faced with challenges.

Example: A project manager facing delays might explore various solutions such as reallocating resources, adjusting timelines, or incorporating new project management tools. Their willingness to experiment and adapt their approach helps them find the most effective way to keep the project on track.

4. Resilience in the Face of Setbacks

The resilience fostered by a growth mindset also contributes to adaptability. When individuals encounter setbacks, they are more likely to persevere and find alternative paths to success.

Example: A startup founder who faces an unexpected market shift might pivot their business model, explore new customer segments, or develop new products in response. Their resilience and adaptability enable the business to survive and thrive despite the challenges.

5. Openness to Feedback and Collaboration

A growth mindset promotes openness to feedback and collaboration. Individuals are more likely to seek out and integrate input from others, which enhances their ability to adapt to new situations and improve their performance.

Example: A software developer working in a collaborative team environment regularly seeks feedback on their code and integrates suggestions to improve it. This openness not only enhances their individual work but also contributes to the overall adaptability and effectiveness of the team.

6. Proactive Approach to Anticipating Future Trends

A growth mindset encourages individuals to be forward-thinking and proactive in anticipating future trends and changes. This anticipation allows them to prepare and adapt more effectively.

Example: A marketing professional who stays informed about emerging digital marketing trends and continuously updates their skills can adapt quickly to new platforms and strategies. This proactive approach ensures that they remain effective and relevant in a rapidly evolving field.

A growth mindset profoundly affects adaptability by fostering a positive and proactive attitude towards change, encouraging continuous learning, promoting flexibility in problem-solving, enhancing resilience, and supporting openness to feedback and collaboration. By embracing change as an opportunity, seeking constant improvement, and being willing to experiment with new approaches, individuals with a growth mindset are better equipped to navigate and thrive in an ever-changing world. This adaptability is essential for personal and professional success in today's dynamic environment.

The Impact of a Growth Mindset on Motivation and Achieving Success

A growth mindset plays a crucial role in enhancing motivation and driving individuals toward achieving success. Here are several ways in which a growth mindset influences motivation and contributes to success, along with examples:

1. Intrinsic Motivation

A growth mindset fosters intrinsic motivation by emphasizing the value of effort and learning over innate talent. Individuals are motivated by the desire to improve and master new skills rather than by external rewards or recognition.

Example: A musician practicing an instrument not for immediate accolades but for the joy of mastering difficult pieces and improving their technical abilities. This intrinsic motivation keeps them committed to their practice and leads to continuous improvement.

2. Goal Setting and Persistence

Individuals with a growth mindset set challenging yet achievable goals. They are more likely to break down larger objectives into smaller, manageable tasks, which helps maintain motivation and focus. They also persist through difficulties, knowing that effort will lead to improvement.

Example: An entrepreneur who sets specific, incremental milestones for their startup. By achieving these smaller goals, they stay motivated and on track to reach their ultimate vision for the company, even when facing setbacks.

3. Embracing Challenges

A growth mindset encourages individuals to embrace challenges as opportunities for growth. This perspective makes them more willing to take on difficult tasks, knowing that overcoming these challenges will lead to personal and professional development.

Example: A student who chooses to enroll in advanced courses despite the increased difficulty because they see the challenge as a chance to expand their knowledge and skills. This willingness to tackle challenging subjects leads to greater academic achievement.

4. Learning from Criticism

Individuals with a growth mindset view feedback and criticism as valuable tools for improvement. This openness to constructive criticism helps them learn from their mistakes and make necessary adjustments, which is essential for long-term success.

Example: An athlete who actively seeks feedback from their coach and teammates to refine their techniques and strategies. By learning from this feedback, they continuously improve their performance and achieve greater success in their sport.

5. Developing a Passion for Learning

A growth mindset instills a passion for learning and self-improvement. This passion drives individuals to seek out new knowledge and skills, which is crucial for staying competitive and achieving success in any field.

Example: A professional who regularly attends workshops, reads industry publications, and pursues additional certifications to stay updated with the latest trends and advancements. This commitment to continuous learning enhances their expertise and career prospects.

6. Building Resilience

Resilience, a key component of a growth mindset, helps individuals stay motivated even when facing setbacks. The belief that they can overcome obstacles through effort and learning keeps them focused on their goals, despite challenges.

Example: A writer who receives multiple rejections from publishers but continues to refine their manuscript based on feedback and persists in submitting their work. Their resilience eventually leads to their book being published and achieving success.

A growth mindset significantly impacts motivation and the pursuit of success by fostering intrinsic motivation, encouraging goal setting and persistence, promoting the embrace of challenges, valuing learning from criticism, developing a passion for learning, and building resilience. By cultivating a growth mindset, individuals are more likely to stay motivated, continuously improve their skills, and ultimately achieve their personal and professional goals. This mindset not only drives immediate progress but also sustains long-term success by instilling a lifelong commitment to growth and self-improvement.

2.3 Share research findings and real-life examples demonstrating the transformative power of adopting a growth mindset

Research Findings and Real-Life Examples of the Transformative Power of a Growth Mindset

Research Findings

Carol Dweck's Pioneering Research

Carol Dweck, a psychologist at Stanford University, is the foremost researcher on growth mindset. Her studies have shown that students who believe their intelligence can be developed (growth mindset) outperform those who believe their intelligence is fixed (fixed mindset). In one study, students were taught that their brains could grow stronger with effort and practice. These students subsequently improved their grades significantly compared to a control group that did not receive this intervention.

Impact on Academic Performance

A study published in "Psychological Science" demonstrated that teaching a growth mindset to students, particularly those at risk of underachievement, significantly improved their grades and standardized test scores. This intervention was particularly effective for minority students and those from low-income backgrounds, highlighting the mindset's role in narrowing achievement gaps.

Employee Performance and Innovation

Research by the consulting firm Bain & Company found that companies fostering a growth mindset among employees were more likely to encourage innovation, creativity, and risk-taking. Employees in these companies reported feeling more empowered and committed to their work, leading to higher performance levels and job satisfaction.

Mental Health and Well-Being

Studies have also linked a growth mindset to better mental health outcomes. Research published in the "Journal of Adolescence" found that adolescents with a growth mindset had lower levels of anxiety and depression. This is because they view challenges as opportunities to learn rather than as threats, reducing stress and improving overall well-being.

Few more research findings

Additional Research Findings on the Transformative Power of a Growth Mindset

1. Educational Interventions and Academic Success

Study by Blackwell, Brzezinski, and Dweck (2007): This landmark study involved junior high school students and found that those who were taught a growth mindset exhibited a significant increase in math grades compared to a control group. The intervention included teaching students that intelligence is malleable and can be developed with effort and perseverance.

Impact on Low-Achieving Students: Research published in the "Journal of Educational Psychology" showed that students who were performing poorly improved significantly after receiving growth mindset training. These interventions helped to close achievement gaps, particularly benefiting students from disadvantaged backgrounds.

2. Workplace Performance and Professional Development

Organizational Mindsets Study: Research by Heslin and VandeWalle (2008) found that managers with a growth mindset are more likely to develop their employees' potential, leading to higher overall team performance. These managers view their employees' skills and abilities as improvable, which encourages a more supportive and developmental work environment.

Employee Engagement and Retention: A study published in "Personnel Psychology" indicated that employees with a growth mindset are more engaged and show higher levels of job satisfaction. They are more likely to embrace new challenges and are less likely to leave the organization, contributing to lower turnover rates and a more stable workforce.

3. Mental Health and Coping Strategies

Mindset and Stress Response: Research published in the "Journal of Personality and Social Psychology" found that individuals with a growth mindset are better at coping with stress. They tend to interpret stressful situations as opportunities to learn and grow, which reduces the psychological impact of stress and improves overall mental health.

Growth Mindset and Depression: A study in "Clinical Psychological Science" showed that interventions promoting a growth mindset can reduce symptoms of depression. By helping individuals reframe their thinking patterns and view challenges as solvable problems, these interventions foster a more positive and proactive approach to mental health.

4. Sports and Physical Performance

Athlete Mindset Study: Research conducted by John G. Nicholls (1984) in the realm of sports psychology found that athletes with a growth mindset are more likely to set challenging goals, engage in deliberate practice, and exhibit resilience in the face of setbacks. These athletes show improved performance and higher levels of achievement in their respective sports.

Impact on Physical Education: A study published in the "Journal of Sport & Exercise Psychology" demonstrated that students with a growth mindset in physical education classes show greater improvements in their physical skills and are more motivated to participate in physical activities.

5. Creativity and Innovation

Creativity and Growth Mindset: Research by Karwowski (2014) in the "Journal of Creative Behavior" found a positive correlation between a growth mindset and creative output. Individuals who believe that their creative abilities can be developed are more likely to engage in creative thinking and problem-solving, leading to higher levels of innovation.

Corporate Innovation: A study in "Research Policy" examined companies that cultivate a growth mindset culture and found that these companies are more innovative. Employees are encouraged to experiment, take risks, and learn from failures, which fosters a culture of continuous improvement and creative problem-solving.

These additional research findings underscore the wide-ranging impact of a growth mindset on various aspects of life, from education and workplace performance to mental health, sports, and creativity. By fostering a belief in the potential for development and improvement, a growth mindset enhances resilience, adaptability, and motivation, leading to greater success and fulfillment in both personal and professional domains.

Real-Life Examples

Michael Jordan: The Basketball Legend

Michael Jordan is often cited as a prime example of a growth mindset. Cut from his high school basketball team, Jordan used this setback as motivation to improve his skills. His relentless work ethic and dedication to practice transformed him into one of the greatest basketball players of all time. Jordan's story exemplifies how viewing failure as a steppingstone can lead to extraordinary success.

J.K. Rowling: The Harry Potter Phenomenon

Before achieving fame with the Harry Potter series, J.K. Rowling faced numerous rejections from publishers. Despite these setbacks, she continued to refine her manuscript and persisted in her efforts. Her belief in her ability to improve and her refusal to be discouraged by failure eventually led to one of the most successful literary careers in history.

Steve Jobs: The Innovator

Steve Jobs' career at Apple showcases the power of a growth mindset in fostering innovation and resilience. After being ousted from the company he co-founded, Jobs did not view this as a final defeat. Instead, he used the experience to grow, founding NeXT and Pixar, which became highly successful. His return to Apple marked the beginning of an era of unprecedented innovation, culminating in products like the iPhone and iPad.

Angela Duckworth's Grit Research

Angela Duckworth's research on grit, which shares similarities with a growth mindset, has shown that perseverance and passion for long-term goals are crucial for success. Her work, summarized in her book "Grit: The Power of Passion and Perseverance," highlights how individuals with a growth mindset exhibit higher levels of grit, leading to greater achievements in various domains, from education to business to athletics.

Satya Nadella: Transforming Microsoft

When Satya Nadella became CEO of Microsoft, he brought a growth mindset to the company, shifting its culture from a "know-it-all" to a "learn-it-all" mentality. This cultural transformation has been credited with revitalizing Microsoft, fostering innovation, and leading to significant growth in areas like cloud computing and AI. Nadella's emphasis on continuous learning and development has had a profound impact on Microsoft's success.

Research findings and real-life examples vividly demonstrate the transformative power of adopting a growth mindset. From improved academic performance and mental health to groundbreaking innovations and personal success stories, the benefits of a growth mindset are far-reaching and profound. By fostering resilience, encouraging continuous learning, and embracing challenges, a growth mindset empowers individuals and organizations to achieve their full potential and drive sustained success.

Summary of Chapter 2: "The Power of Growth Mindset"

2.1 Explore deep into the characteristics and benefits of a growth-oriented mindset:

In this section, the chapter delves into the core principles of a growth mindset, emphasizing its fundamental characteristics and the benefits it offers. It highlights how individuals with a growth mindset believe that abilities and intelligence can be developed through dedication and hard work. This mindset fosters a love for learning and resilience in the face of challenges. The section also explores the contrast with a fixed mindset, where abilities are seen as innate and unchangeable, limiting personal growth and achievement.

2.2 Discuss how embracing a growth mindset leads to increased resilience, adaptability, and motivation:

This part of the chapter explores the practical implications of adopting a growth mindset. It discusses how individuals who embrace this mindset are better equipped to navigate setbacks and failures. They view challenges as opportunities for growth rather than obstacles to overcome. This perspective enhances their resilience, enabling them to bounce back stronger after setbacks. Moreover, a growth mindset promotes adaptability by encouraging continuous learning and improvement. It fuels intrinsic motivation, as individuals focus on mastering skills and achieving personal development rather than seeking external validation.

2.3 Share research findings and real-life examples demonstrating the transformative power of adopting a growth mindset:

The final section of the chapter presents empirical evidence and real-life stories that illustrate the transformative impact of a growth mindset. Drawing from psychological research and case studies, it showcases how individuals, teams, and organizations have achieved remarkable success by cultivating a growth-oriented perspective. These examples highlight instances where individuals have overcome significant challenges, achieved breakthroughs, and reach new heights by embracing the belief that their abilities can be developed over time.

Overall, Chapter 2 aims to inspire readers to adopt and nurture a growth mindset, demonstrating its profound influence on personal and professional development. It encourages readers to reflect on their own mindset and consider how embracing a growth-oriented perspective can unlock their full potential.

"A growth mindset is the key that unlocks the door to endless possibilities, turning challenges into steppingstones and dreams into reality." – Author

Key Takeaways

2.1 Explore deep into the characteristics and benefits of a growth-oriented mindset:

Core Characteristics: A growth mindset involves believing that abilities and intelligence can be developed through effort, learning, and perseverance.

Benefits: It fosters a love for learning, resilience in the face of challenges, and a focus on continuous improvement.

Contrast with Fixed Mindset: Contrasts with a fixed mindset where abilities are seen as innate and unchangeable, limiting personal growth.

2.2 Discuss how embracing a growth mindset leads to increased resilience, adaptability, and motivation:

Resilience: Individuals with a growth mindset view setbacks as opportunities for learning and growth, leading to greater resilience.

Adaptability: It promotes adaptability by encouraging individuals to embrace change and seek opportunities for improvement.

Motivation: Focuses on intrinsic motivation, driven by the desire to master skills and achieve personal development rather than seeking external validation.

2.3 Share research findings and real-life examples demonstrating the transformative power of adopting a growth mindset:

Empirical Evidence: Research demonstrates that adopting a growth mindset leads to higher achievement, improved relationships, and greater well-being.

Real-life Examples: Stories illustrate how individuals, teams, and organizations have overcome challenges and achieved success through perseverance and a belief in continuous improvement.

Transformation: Shows how adopting a growth mindset can transform individuals' lives and organizational cultures, unlocking their full potential.

These key takeaways emphasize the practical benefits and transformative impact of embracing a growth mindset, encouraging readers to reflect on their own mindset and consider how they can cultivate a more growth-oriented perspective in their personal and professional lives.

Action Steps

2.1 Explore deep into the characteristics and benefits of a growth-oriented mindset:

Reflect and Identify: Take time to reflect on your current beliefs about abilities and intelligence. Identify areas where you might hold a fixed mindset versus a growth mindset.

Cultivate Growth Mentality: Start cultivating a growth mindset by embracing challenges as opportunities to learn and grow. Set learning goals that challenge you to develop new skills.

Seek Feedback: Embrace feedback as a tool for improvement rather than criticism. Actively seek constructive feedback to help you develop and grow.

2.2 Discuss how embracing a growth mindset leads to increased resilience, adaptability, and motivation:

Develop Resilience: When faced with setbacks or challenges, remind yourself that setbacks are part of the learning process. Focus on what you can learn from the experience and how you can grow stronger as a result.

Embrace Change: Practice adapting to change by approaching new situations with a curiosity for learning and improvement. Challenge yourself to see change as an opportunity for personal and professional growth.

Set Intrinsic Goals: Identify intrinsic motivations that drive you to excel in your pursuits. Set goals that focus on mastering skills and achieving personal growth rather than external recognition.

2.3 Share research findings and real-life examples demonstrating the transformative power of adopting a growth mindset:

Study Success Stories: Study real-life examples of individuals or organizations that have embraced a growth mindset to achieve success. Draw inspiration from their journeys and apply similar principles to your own goals.

Apply Research Insights: Use research findings on growth mindset to inform your approach to personal and professional development. Integrate evidence-based strategies into your daily routines and practices.

Practice Continuous Improvement: Commit to a mindset of continuous improvement by regularly evaluating your progress and adjusting your goals. Celebrate small victories and learn from setbacks to fuel your ongoing growth journey.

These action steps are designed to help you actively cultivate a growth mindset, enhance your resilience and adaptability, and fuel your intrinsic motivation for learning and development. By implementing these strategies, you can harness the transformative power of a growth-oriented perspective in both your personal and professional life.

In Chapter 2, we explored the profound impact of a growth mindset on personal development and achievement. We delved into the core characteristics and numerous benefits of embracing a growth-oriented perspective, highlighting how it enhances resilience, adaptability, and motivation in the face of challenges. Through a synthesis of research findings and real-life success stories, we witnessed firsthand the transformative power of adopting a growth mindset, illustrating its ability to catalyze personal growth and unlock untapped potential."

"Now, in Chapter 3, we shift our focus to overcoming self-limiting beliefs that often hinder progress and success. Here, we identify and dissect common barriers that impede personal growth, offering practical strategies and exercises to challenge and reframe negative thoughts. By cultivating self-awareness and nurturing a positive, empowering mindset, readers will gain invaluable tools to break free from limiting beliefs and unleash their full potential. This chapter serves as a roadmap for self-discovery and transformation, guiding readers toward a mindset that fosters resilience, fosters growth, and paves the way for lasting success.

Chapter 3: Overcoming Self-Limiting Beliefs

"The only thing standing between you and your goal is the story you keep telling yourself as to why you can't achieve it."

— Jordan Belfort

A short story

In the ancient epic of Ramayana, one of the most poignant stories illustrating the power of mindset unfolds during Lord Rama's exile in the forest. Accompanied by his devoted wife Sita and loyal brother Lakshmana, Rama faced numerous trials and tribulations that tested his resilience and determination.

One such instance occurred when the demon king Ravana, driven by his desire for Sita, abducted her and took her to his kingdom of Lanka. Distraught and determined to rescue his beloved wife, Rama embarked on an arduous journey filled with challenges and obstacles.

During his search, Rama encountered Hanuman, the mighty monkey warrior and devotee of Lord Rama. Hanuman pledged his allegiance to Rama and became instrumental in the quest to find Sita. Hanuman's unwavering faith in Lord Rama and his determination to fulfill his duty as a servant of righteousness exemplify the power of a steadfast mindset.

Hanuman's mindset was characterized by unwavering devotion, unyielding courage, and undeterred focus on his mission. Despite facing formidable adversaries and daunting hurdles, Hanuman remained resolute in his resolve to locate Sita and deliver Rama's message of hope and reassurance to her.

Through his extraordinary feats of strength, intelligence, and devotion, Hanuman demonstrated that a focused and determined mindset can overcome seemingly insurmountable challenges. His unwavering faith in the righteousness of his cause and his commitment to serving Rama's purpose serve as timeless lessons in courage, dedication, and the transformative power of mindset.

In the journey depicted in Ramayana, Hanuman's story inspires us to cultivate a mindset characterized by determination, resilience, and unwavering faith in our abilities and principles. It reminds us that with the right mindset, fueled by courage and conviction, we can navigate life's trials and achieve our goals with clarity and purpose.

3.1 Identify Common Self-Limiting Beliefs That Hinder Personal Growth and Success

Understanding Self-Limiting Beliefs: Self-limiting beliefs are negative thoughts that restrict a person's potential. They often stem from past experiences, societal expectations, and fear of failure.

Examples of Self-Limiting Beliefs:

"I'm not good enough to achieve this."

"Success is only for lucky people, not for me."

"I can't change because this is just who I am."

Impact on Personal Growth: These beliefs can lead to procrastination, low self-esteem, and avoidance of new opportunities, ultimately stalling personal and professional development.

Root Causes: Exploring the origins of these beliefs, such as childhood experiences, cultural norms, and past failures, helps in understanding their impact on one's mindset.

3.2 Offer Practical Strategies and Exercises for Challenging and Reframing Negative Thoughts and Beliefs

Self-Awareness: The first step in overcoming self-limiting beliefs is to become aware of them. Regular self-reflection and journaling can help identify these negative thoughts.

Challenging Beliefs: Question the validity of self-limiting beliefs by asking:

"Is this belief based on facts or assumptions?"

"What evidence do I have that contradicts this belief?"

"How would my life be different if I didn't hold this belief?"

Reframing Techniques: Replace negative beliefs with positive, empowering ones. For example, change "I'm not good enough" to "I am capable of learning and improving."

Affirmations: Use daily affirmations to reinforce positive beliefs. Statements like "I am capable and deserving of success" can help rewire the brain for positivity.

Visualization: Visualize successful outcomes to build confidence and reduce the power of negative beliefs.

Professional Help: Sometimes, seeking guidance from a coach or therapist can provide additional support in overcoming deeply ingrained self-limiting beliefs.

3.3 Provide Guidance on Building Self-Awareness and Cultivating a Positive, Empowering Mindset

Mindfulness Practices: Engage in mindfulness activities like meditation and deep-breathing exercises to stay present and aware of negative thought patterns.

Regular Reflection: Set aside time for regular reflection to assess progress in overcoming self-limiting beliefs and to celebrate small victories.

Gratitude Journal: Keeping a gratitude journal helps shift focus from what's lacking to what's abundant, fostering a positive outlook.

Surround Yourself with Positivity: Engage with supportive, positive individuals who encourage growth and challenge negative thinking.

Continuous Learning: Embrace lifelong learning to build competence and confidence, which naturally diminishes the impact of self-limiting beliefs.

Setting Realistic Goals: Break down large goals into smaller, achievable steps to build confidence and maintain motivation.

Celebrate Progress: Acknowledge and celebrate progress, no matter how small, to reinforce the belief that change is possible and happening.

By identifying self-limiting beliefs, challenging and reframing them, and building self-awareness, individuals can cultivate a positive, empowering mindset that paves the way for personal and professional growth. This chapter equips readers with the tools and strategies to break free from the constraints of negative thinking and unlock their full potential.

3.1 Identify common self-limiting beliefs that hinder personal growth and success

Understanding Self-Limiting Beliefs

Self-limiting beliefs are ingrained negative thoughts and perceptions that individuals hold about themselves, which restrict their ability to achieve personal and professional growth. These beliefs often originate from past experiences, societal influences, and a fear of failure.

Examples of Self-Limiting Beliefs

1. "I'm Not Good Enough to Achieve This."

Example: Sarah, a talented writer, consistently avoids submitting her work to publishers because she believes her writing is not up to par. Despite positive feedback from peers, she is paralyzed by the fear of rejection and failure.

Research Insight: According to a study by Bandura (1977) on self-efficacy, individuals with low self-efficacy are less likely to pursue challenging tasks and more likely to give up when facing obstacles.

2. "Success is Only for Lucky People, Not for Me."

Example: John, an aspiring entrepreneur, hesitates to start his own business because he believes success is a matter of luck rather than effort and skill. He attributes the success of others to external factors like connections and timing, rather than hard work and persistence.

Research Insight: A study by Furnham and Cheng (2015) found that individuals with an external locus of control, who attribute success to luck or fate, are less likely to engage in proactive behaviors that lead to success.

3. "I Can't Change Because This is Just Who I Am."

Example: Emily, a middle-aged professional, feels stuck in her career. She believes her personality traits are fixed and that she cannot develop new skills or adapt to new roles. This belief prevents her from seeking promotions or exploring new career paths.

Research Insight: Carol Dweck's research on fixed and growth mindsets (2006) highlights that individuals with a fixed mindset believe their abilities and intelligence are static, which inhibits their willingness to take on new challenges and learn from experiences.

Impact on Personal Growth

These self-limiting beliefs can lead to:

Procrastination: Individuals delay pursuing their goals due to fear of failure or not meeting their own high standards.

Low Self-Esteem: Constant negative self-talk undermines confidence and self-worth, making it difficult to take risks.

Avoidance of Opportunities: Fear of failure or rejection leads individuals to avoid new opportunities, limiting their growth and potential.

Stalled Personal Development: By adhering to these negative beliefs, individuals are unable to recognize their true potential and capabilities, hindering personal and professional development.

Root Causes

Understanding the origins of self-limiting beliefs can help in addressing them:

Childhood Experiences: Negative feedback or criticism during formative years can create lasting impressions of inadequacy.

Cultural Norms: Societal expectations and stereotypes can reinforce self-limiting beliefs, particularly regarding gender roles and career choices.

Past Failures: Previous unsuccessful attempts can lead to generalized beliefs about one's abilities, discouraging future efforts.

Fear of the Unknown: Uncertainty about outcomes can make individuals hesitant to step out of their comfort zones.

Research Articles

Bandura, A. (1977). Self-efficacy: Toward a unifying theory of behavioral change. Psychological Review, 84(2), 191-215.

This study introduces the concept of self-efficacy and its impact on behavior, illustrating how beliefs about one's capabilities affect their willingness to take on challenges and persist in the face of adversity.

Furnham, A., & Cheng, H. (2015). The role of locus of control and self-efficacy in predicting career satisfaction: A review and meta-analysis. Journal of Career Assessment, 23(3), 283-299.

This research examines how individuals' beliefs about control over their life outcomes influence their career satisfaction and proactive behaviors.

Dweck, C. S. (2006). Mindset: The New Psychology of Success. Random House.

Dweck's seminal work on fixed and growth mindsets provides insight into how beliefs about the malleability of abilities affect motivation, learning, and achievement.

By identifying and understanding these common self-limiting beliefs, individuals can begin to challenge and overcome them, paving the way for greater personal and professional growth.

3.2 Offer practical strategies and exercises for challenging and reframing negative thoughts and beliefs

Understanding the Importance of Challenging Self-Limiting Beliefs

To overcome self-limiting beliefs, it is essential to challenge and reframe these negative thoughts. This process involves recognizing the harmful patterns of thinking, questioning their validity, and replacing them with more positive and empowering beliefs. Here are some practical strategies and exercises to help achieve this transformation.

Practical Strategies

1. Self-Awareness and Reflection

Strategy: Develop self-awareness by regularly reflecting on your thoughts and behaviors. Keep a journal to document instances when you notice negative self-talk or limiting beliefs.

Exercise: Spend 10 minutes each day writing about your experiences and noting any recurring negative thoughts. Reflect on the situations that trigger these thoughts and how they impact your behavior.

2. Cognitive Restructuring

Strategy: Cognitive restructuring involves identifying and challenging irrational or negative thoughts and replacing them with more balanced and realistic ones.

Exercise: Use the ABC model (Antecedent, Belief, Consequence) to analyze a recent event where you experienced a limiting belief. Write down the triggering event (Antecedent), the negative thought (Belief), and the resulting emotion or behavior (Consequence). Then, challenge the belief by asking questions such as:

Is this belief based on facts or assumptions?

What evidence supports or contradicts this belief?

How would I advise a friend in a similar situation?

3. Positive Affirmations

Strategy: Positive affirmations are statements that reinforce positive self-beliefs and counteract negative thinking. Repeating affirmations can help reprogram the subconscious mind.

Exercise: Create a list of positive affirmations that address your self-limiting beliefs. For example, if you believe you are not capable of success, an affirmation could be, "I am capable and deserving of success." Repeat these affirmations daily, preferably in front of a mirror, to reinforce the positive messages.

4. Visualization Techniques

Strategy: Visualization involves creating a mental image of a desired outcome, which can help reinforce positive beliefs and motivate action.

Exercise: Spend a few minutes each day visualizing yourself achieving a specific goal. Imagine the steps you take, the obstacles you overcome, and the positive emotions you feel. This practice can help build confidence and reduce anxiety related to self-limiting beliefs.

5. Goal Setting and Action Planning

Strategy: Setting realistic and achievable goals can help you build confidence and challenge self-limiting beliefs.

Exercise: Break down a larger goal into smaller, manageable steps. For each step, identify specific actions you need to take and set a timeline. Celebrate small victories along the way to reinforce your belief in your abilities.

6. Mindfulness and Meditation

Strategy: Mindfulness and meditation practices can help you become more aware of your thoughts and reduce the impact of negative thinking.

Exercise: Practice mindfulness meditation for 10-15 minutes each day. Focus on your breath and observe your thoughts without judgment. When negative thoughts arise, acknowledge them and gently bring your focus back to your breath. Over time, this practice can help you develop a more balanced perspective.

7. Seeking Support from Others

Strategy: Engaging with supportive friends, family, or a mentor can provide encouragement and different perspectives on your self-limiting beliefs.

Exercise: Share your experiences and challenges with someone you trust. Ask for their feedback and support in challenging your negative thoughts. Consider joining a support group or seeking professional counseling if needed.

Practical Exercises

1. Thought Record Exercise

Purpose: To identify and challenge negative thoughts.

Steps:

Identify a specific situation that triggered a negative thought.

Write down the thought and rate its intensity on a scale of 1-10.

Challenge the thought by asking questions such as, "What evidence supports this thought?" and "What evidence contradicts it?"

Replace the negative thought with a more balanced one and rate its intensity.

2. Reframing Negative Thoughts Exercise

Purpose: To practice changing negative thoughts into positive ones.

Steps:

List common negative thoughts you experience.

For each negative thought, write a positive reframe. For example, change "I always fail" to "I learn from my mistakes and improve."

Practice repeating the positive reframes regularly.

3. Success Journal Exercise

Purpose: To build confidence by focusing on past successes.

Steps:

Keep a journal where you record daily achievements and positive experiences, no matter how small.

Reflect on these entries regularly to reinforce your belief in your abilities and potential for success.

Research Articles Supporting These Strategies

Burns, D. D. (1980). Feeling Good: The New Mood Therapy.

This book explains cognitive behavioral therapy techniques, including cognitive restructuring, which can be used to challenge and reframe negative thoughts.

Seligman, M. E. P. (1990). Learned Optimism: How to Change Your Mind and Your Life.

Seligman's work explores the impact of positive thinking and optimism on personal well-being and success.

Carver, C. S., & Scheier, M. F. (1998). On the Self-Regulation of Behavior.

This book provides insights into goal setting and self-regulation strategies that can help individuals overcome self-limiting beliefs.

By implementing these practical strategies and exercises, individuals can effectively challenge and reframe their self-limiting beliefs, paving the way for personal growth and success.

3 more strategies for Challenging and Reframing Negative Thoughts and Beliefs

1. Gratitude Practice

Strategy: Cultivating gratitude can shift your focus from negative thoughts to positive aspects of your life, helping to counteract self-limiting beliefs.

Exercise:

Gratitude Journal: Each day, write down three things you are grateful for. These can be small or significant events, interactions, or personal achievements. Reflecting on these entries regularly can help reframe your mindset towards positivity.

Gratitude Letter: Write a letter to someone you appreciate, detailing why you are grateful for them and the impact they have had on your life. Even if you don't send the letter, this exercise can help reinforce positive thoughts and reduce negative self-talk.

2. Strengths Identification

Strategy: Recognizing and leveraging your strengths can boost self-confidence and challenge negative self-perceptions.

Exercise:

Strengths Inventory: Make a list of your strengths and accomplishments. Think about times when you successfully used these strengths. Review this list regularly to remind yourself of your capabilities.

Strengths Application: Identify a current challenge or goal and plan how you can use your strengths to address it. This can help you approach obstacles with a positive and proactive mindset.

3. Role Models and Mentorship

Strategy: Learning from role models and seeking mentorship can provide guidance and inspiration, helping to overcome self-limiting beliefs.

Exercise:

Identify Role Models: List people you admire who have overcome challenges similar to yours. Research their stories to understand how they navigated their obstacles and maintained a positive mindset.

Seek a Mentor: Find a mentor who can offer advice, support, and constructive feedback. Regularly meet with your mentor to discuss your goals, challenges, and progress. Their insights can help you reframe negative thoughts and develop a more resilient mindset.

Research Articles Supporting These Strategies

Emmons, R. A., & McCullough, M. E. (2003). Counting blessings versus burdens: An experimental investigation of gratitude and subjective well-being in daily life. Journal of Personality and Social Psychology, 84(2), 377-389.

This study shows how practicing gratitude can enhance well-being and reduce negative thinking.

Clifton, D. O., & Harter, J. K. (2003). Investing in strengths. In K. S. Cameron, J. E. Dutton, & R. E. Quinn (Eds.), Positive organizational scholarship: Foundations of a new discipline (pp. 111-121). Berrett-Koehler.

This chapter explains the benefits of identifying and leveraging personal strengths in various aspects of life.

Kram, K. E. (1985). Mentoring at work: Developmental relationships in organizational life. University Press of America.

This book discusses the importance of mentorship and its impact on personal and professional development.

By integrating these additional strategies into your daily routine, you can further challenge and reframe self-limiting beliefs, fostering a more positive and resilient mindset.

3.3 Provide guidance on building self-awareness and cultivating a positive, empowering mindset

Building Self-Awareness

Strategy: Mindfulness Practice

Exercise:

Mindful Breathing: Set aside a few minutes each day to focus on your breath. Notice the sensation of each inhale and exhale without judgment. This practice can help you become more aware of your thoughts and emotions as they arise.

Body Scan: Conduct a body scan meditation where you systematically focus your attention on different parts of your body. This practice enhances awareness of physical sensations and promotes relaxation.

Strategy: Journaling

Exercise:

Daily Reflection: Spend time each evening reflecting on your day. Write down your thoughts, feelings, and any patterns you notice in your behavior. This practice encourages introspection and helps identify areas for personal growth.

Gratitude Journal: In addition to fostering gratitude, a journal can help you become more aware of positive aspects of your life, fostering a more optimistic mindset.

Cultivating a Positive, Empowering Mindset

Strategy: Affirmations and Positive Self-Talk

Exercise:

Daily Affirmations: Create positive statements about yourself and your abilities. Repeat these affirmations regularly, especially during challenging times. This practice can reshape your self-perception and boost confidence.

Challenge Negative Thoughts: When negative thoughts arise, counter them with positive affirmations or realistic perspectives. For example, if you catch yourself thinking "I can't do this," replace it with "I am capable and have overcome challenges before."

Strategy: Setting and Achieving Goals

Exercise:

SMART Goals: Set Specific, Measurable, Achievable, Relevant, and Time-bound goals. Break down larger goals into smaller, manageable steps. Tracking your progress reinforces a sense of accomplishment and motivates further action.

Celebrate Milestones: Recognize and celebrate your achievements, no matter how small. This practice reinforces positive behavior and encourages continued effort towards your goals.

Research Articles Supporting These Strategies

Brown, K. W., & Ryan, R. M. (2003). The benefits of being present: Mindfulness and its role in psychological well-being. Journal of Personality and Social Psychology, 84(4), 822-848.

This article explores how mindfulness practices enhance self-awareness and overall well-being.

Wood, J. V., Perunovic, W. Q., & Lee, J. W. (2009). Positive self-statements: Power for some, peril for others. Psychological Science, 20(7), 860-866.

This study discusses the effectiveness of positive self-talk in cultivating a positive mindset.

Locke, E. A., & Latham, G. P. (2002). Building a practically useful theory of goal setting and task motivation: A 35-year odyssey. American Psychologist, 57(9), 705-717.

This research provides insights into effective goal-setting strategies that promote motivation and achievement.

By integrating these guidance and exercises into your daily routine, you can enhance self-awareness, cultivate a positive mindset, and empower yourself to navigate challenges with resilience and optimism.

10 strategies for building self-awareness:

Mindfulness Meditation:

Practice mindfulness meditation regularly to cultivate present-moment awareness of thoughts, emotions, and sensations without judgment.

Journaling:

Keep a daily journal to reflect on your thoughts, feelings, and experiences. This practice enhances self-reflection and insight.

Self-Reflection Exercises:

Set aside time periodically to ask yourself reflective questions about your goals, values, and aspirations. Write down your answers to gain deeper understanding.

Feedback Solicitation:

Seek feedback from trusted friends, family members, or mentors about your strengths, weaknesses, and areas for improvement. Use their perspectives to gain insight into yourself.

Psychological Assessments:

Take personality assessments or psychological tests, such as Myers-Briggs Type Indicator (MBTI) or StrengthsFinder, to understand your personality traits and strengths.

Body Awareness Practices:

Engage in practices like yoga, tai chi, or body scan meditation to enhance awareness of physical sensations and tensions in your body.

Mindful Eating:

Practice mindful eating by paying attention to the taste, texture, and sensations of each bite. This helps cultivate awareness of your relationship with food and eating habits.

Artistic Expression:

Express yourself through creative activities like painting, writing, or music. Artistic expression can reveal subconscious thoughts and emotions.

Daily Mindful Moments:

Incorporate mindfulness into everyday activities such as walking, showering, or commuting. Focus on the present moment and observe your thoughts and surroundings.

Therapeutic Techniques:

Explore therapeutic techniques such as cognitive behavioral therapy (CBT), dialectical behavior therapy (DBT), or introspective practices guided by a therapist or counselor.

These strategies can be tailored to your preferences and lifestyle to deepen self-awareness, enhance personal growth, and foster a greater understanding of yourself and your interactions with the world.

10 strategies for cultivating a positive empowering mindset.

Practice Gratitude Daily:

Start or end your day by writing down three things you're grateful for. This helps shift focus to positive aspects of life and fosters a sense of appreciation.

Affirmations and Positive Self-Talk:

Use affirmations to reinforce positive beliefs about yourself and your abilities. Replace negative self-talk with affirming statements to boost confidence and self-esteem.

Visualize Success:

Visualize achieving your goals and visualize yourself overcoming challenges. This mental rehearsal can enhance motivation and belief in your capabilities.

Set SMART Goals:

Set Specific, Measurable, Achievable, Relevant, and Time-bound (SMART) goals. Break them down into smaller tasks and celebrate progress to maintain motivation.

Surround Yourself with Positive Influences:

Spend time with supportive and optimistic people who encourage your growth and success. Their positivity can inspire and uplift you.

Learn from Challenges:

View setbacks and challenges as opportunities for growth and learning. Embrace failure as a steppingstone toward success rather than a deterrent.

Practice Mindfulness and Presence:

Cultivate mindfulness by focusing on the present moment. This reduces stress, enhances clarity, and promotes a positive outlook on life.

Take Care of Your Physical Health:

Prioritize regular exercise, nutritious eating, and sufficient sleep. Physical well-being significantly impacts mental and emotional resilience.

Challenge Negative Thoughts:

Challenge and reframe negative thoughts by questioning their validity and considering alternative perspectives. Replace them with more realistic and positive interpretations.

Celebrate Small Wins:

Acknowledge and celebrate your achievements, no matter how small. Recognizing progress reinforces a sense of accomplishment and boosts motivation.

By integrating these strategies into your daily life, you can cultivate a positive and empowering mindset that supports resilience, growth, and a greater sense of well-being.

Summary of Chapter 3: Overcoming Self-Limiting Beliefs

In Chapter 3, we explored the intricate aspects of self-limiting beliefs, recognizing their profound impact on personal growth and success.

3.1 Identifying Common Self-Limiting Beliefs:

This section begins by identifying pervasive self-limiting beliefs that often hinder individuals from reaching their full potential. Examples include beliefs like "I'm not smart enough," "I don't deserve success," or "I'm too old to start something new." By understanding these beliefs, readers can recognize their influence on behaviors and outcomes, paving the way for transformative change.

3.2 Strategies for Challenging and Reframing Negative Thoughts:

Practical strategies are offered to challenge and reframe negative thoughts and beliefs. Techniques such as cognitive restructuring, where individuals question the validity and accuracy of their negative beliefs, are introduced. Exercises include journaling to track negative thoughts, replacing them with positive affirmations, and seeking evidence that contradicts these limiting beliefs. By actively engaging in these exercises, readers can shift their mindset towards more empowering beliefs that support growth and achievement.

3.3 Guidance on Building Self-Awareness and Cultivating a Positive Mindset:

This section provides actionable guidance on building self-awareness and cultivating a positive, empowering mindset. It emphasizes the importance of mindfulness practices, such as meditation and self-reflection, to enhance awareness of thought patterns and emotional responses. Strategies also include setting clear goals aligned with personal values, fostering a supportive environment, and practicing self-compassion. By integrating these practices into daily life, readers can develop resilience, enhance self-confidence, and embrace a mindset conducive to personal fulfillment and success.

In essence, Chapter 3 equips readers with the tools to identify, challenge, and overcome self-limiting beliefs, empowering them to cultivate a mindset that fosters growth, resilience, and positive transformation.

Key Takeaways

3.1 Identifying Common Self-Limiting Beliefs:

Recognize the pervasive nature of self-limiting beliefs that hinder personal growth and success.

Examples include beliefs about inadequacy, limitations based on age or past experiences.

Understanding these beliefs is crucial for initiating change and personal transformation.

3.2 Strategies for Challenging and Reframing Negative Thoughts:

Engage in cognitive restructuring by questioning the validity and accuracy of negative beliefs.

Use journaling to track negative thoughts and replace them with affirmations and positive self-talk.

Seek evidence that contradicts self-limiting beliefs to build confidence and shift mindset towards empowerment.

3.3 Guidance on Building Self-Awareness and Cultivating a Positive Mindset:

Practice mindfulness techniques such as meditation and self-reflection to enhance self-awareness.

Set meaningful goals aligned with personal values to foster a sense of purpose and direction.

Create a supportive environment that encourages growth and resilience.

Practice self-compassion and kindness towards oneself to build emotional strength and confidence.

These key takeaways from Chapter 3 provide actionable insights and strategies for overcoming self-limiting beliefs, cultivating self-awareness, and fostering a positive mindset conducive to personal growth and success.

Action Steps

3.1 Identifying Common Self-Limiting Beliefs:

Self-Assessment: Reflect on personal beliefs that may be limiting your growth and success. Write down specific thoughts that come to mind when facing challenges.

Identify Patterns: Notice recurring themes in your self-limiting beliefs, such as fears of failure or feelings of inadequacy.

External Validation: Seek feedback from trusted friends, mentors, or coaches to identify blind spots and gain perspective on your beliefs.

3.2 Strategies for Challenging and Reframing Negative Thoughts:

Thought Monitoring: Start a journal to record negative thoughts as they arise. Include the situation triggering the thought and how it makes you feel.

Cognitive Restructuring: Challenge negative thoughts by questioning their validity. Ask yourself, "Is there evidence to support this belief? What would I say to a friend in a similar situation?"

Affirmations: Develop positive affirmations that counteract each self-limiting belief identified. Repeat these affirmations daily to reinforce new empowering beliefs.

3.3 Guidance on Building Self-Awareness and Cultivating a Positive Mindset:

Mindfulness Practice: Dedicate time each day to mindfulness activities such as meditation or deep breathing exercises. Focus on observing thoughts and emotions without judgment.

Goal Setting: Define short-term and long-term goals that align with your values and aspirations. Break down larger goals into smaller, manageable steps to track progress.

Environment Optimization: Surround yourself with supportive individuals who uplift and encourage personal growth. Minimize exposure to environments that reinforce negative beliefs.

These action steps are designed to help you proactively address self-limiting beliefs, cultivate self-awareness, and develop a positive mindset conducive to personal empowerment and growth.

"To overcome self-limiting beliefs is to embrace the truth that our greatest barriers are often the ones we create within our own minds." – Author

In Chapter 3, we embarked on a journey to confront and conquer self-limiting beliefs that obstruct personal growth and success. We identified pervasive beliefs that often act as barriers, hindering our journey towards fulfillment. Through practical strategies and exercises, we learned how to challenge and reframe these negative thoughts, paving the way for a transformative shift in mindset. Building on this foundation, we explored the importance of self-awareness and the cultivation of a positive, empowering mindset. These insights serve as catalysts for personal development, empowering readers to harness their inner strength and unlock their true potential."

In Chapter 4, we go deeper into the dynamics of a growth mindset—a mindset characterized by resilience, adaptability, and an unwavering commitment to learning and improvement. Here, we uncover techniques for fostering a growth-oriented perspective not only within ourselves but also in others, fostering environments conducive to personal and collective growth. We examine the pivotal roles of effort, persistence, and embracing failure as essential components of the growth mindset journey. Additionally, we provide actionable tips for creating supportive communities and environments that nurture continuous development and encourage individuals to thrive. Chapter 4 is a roadmap for cultivating resilience, embracing challenges, and fostering a mindset that champions growth and achievement.

Chapter 4: Cultivating a Growth Mindset

"It does not matter how slowly you go as long as you do not stop."

– Confucius

Twenty strategies to cultivate a growth mindset:

Embrace Challenges: See challenges as opportunities to learn and grow rather than obstacles to avoid.

Learn from Criticism: View feedback and criticism as constructive opportunities for improvement rather than personal attacks.

Set Learning Goals: Focus on developing new skills and acquiring knowledge rather than solely on achieving specific outcomes.

Persist in the Face of Setbacks: See setbacks and failures as temporary and opportunities to learn and try again.

Use the Power of "Yet": Instead of saying "I can't do this," say "I can't do this yet," acknowledging potential for growth and improvement.

Celebrate Effort: Value effort and perseverance over innate talent or immediate success.

Seek Inspiration: Surround yourself with individuals who demonstrate a growth mindset and learn from their experiences and attitudes.

Practice Self-Reflection: Regularly reflect on your progress, strengths, and areas for improvement to foster continuous learning and development.

Challenge Fixed Beliefs: Challenge and replace fixed mindset beliefs with growth-oriented perspectives through awareness and intentional effort.

Use Growth-Oriented Language: Pay attention to the language you use about yourself and others, focusing on potential, progress, and development rather than limitations.

Learn from Others: Study the journeys of successful individuals or role models who have demonstrated resilience and growth mindset principles.

Expand Your Comfort Zone: Regularly challenge yourself to step outside your comfort zone and take on new experiences or tasks.

Practice Mindfulness: Develop awareness of your thoughts and reactions, and consciously choose to approach challenges with a growth mindset.

Use Failure as Feedback: View failures as opportunities to learn valuable lessons and adjust your approach rather than as indications of personal inadequacy.

Develop a Growth Mindset Mantra: Create and repeat affirmations or statements that reinforce your belief in growth and development.

Engage in Lifelong Learning: Cultivate a habit of continuous learning by seeking out new knowledge, skills, and experiences.

Encourage Others: Support and encourage others in their efforts to develop a growth mindset, fostering a positive and collaborative environment.

Focus on the Process: Emphasize the importance of effort, strategies, and perseverance in achieving goals, rather than solely on outcomes.

Visualize Success: Visualize yourself overcoming challenges and achieving your goals, reinforcing a belief in your ability to grow and succeed.

Create a Growth Mindset Action Plan: Develop a personalized plan with specific goals and actionable steps to consistently practice and reinforce growth mindset principles in your daily life.

4.1 Explore techniques for fostering a growth-oriented mindset in oneself and others

Fostering a growth-oriented mindset, both in oneself and others, involves cultivating attitudes and behaviors that prioritize learning, resilience, and continuous improvement. Here are some important techniques for fostering a growth-oriented mindset:

For Oneself:

Embrace Challenges: Seek out challenges that push you out of your comfort zone. View these challenges as opportunities to learn and grow rather than obstacles to avoid.

Learn from Failures: Instead of being discouraged by failures, analyze them for lessons. Understand what went wrong, what can be improved, and how you can approach similar situations differently in the future.

Set Learning Goals: Focus on setting goals that emphasize personal growth and skill development rather than purely outcome-based goals. Break down larger goals into smaller, manageable steps to track progress and celebrate achievements along the way.

Practice Self-Compassion: Be kind and supportive to yourself during setbacks or when facing challenges. Recognize that setbacks are a normal part of the learning process and an opportunity for growth.

Seek Feedback: Actively seek feedback from others to gain insights into your strengths and areas for improvement. Use feedback constructively to adjust your approach and enhance your skills.

Cultivate Curiosity: Approach new situations with curiosity and a willingness to learn. Ask questions, explore different perspectives, and continuously seek opportunities to expand your knowledge and understanding.

Develop Resilience: Build resilience by reframing setbacks as temporary and surmountable obstacles. Focus on developing coping strategies and adaptive responses to challenges.

Challenge Fixed Mindsets: Identify and challenge fixed mindset beliefs about intelligence, abilities, and potential. Cultivate a belief that skills and qualities can be developed through dedication and effort.

Celebrate Growth: Acknowledge and celebrate your progress and achievements, no matter how small. Reflect on how far you've come and recognize the effort and determination that led to your growth.

Practice Gratitude: Cultivate a mindset of gratitude for opportunities to learn and grow. Appreciate the support and resources that contribute to your personal and professional development.

For Others:

Promote a Growth Mindset Culture: Create an environment that values effort, persistence, and learning. Encourage individuals to take risks and embrace challenges without fear of judgment or failure.

Provide Constructive Feedback: Offer specific and constructive feedback that focuses on effort, progress, and areas for improvement rather than fixed traits or outcomes.

Model Growth Mindset Behaviors: Lead by example by demonstrating a growth mindset in your own actions and responses to challenges. Share stories of your own failures and successes to normalize the learning process.

Encourage Collaboration: Foster collaboration and teamwork where individuals can learn from each other's strengths and experiences. Encourage peer mentoring and support networks.

Offer Growth Opportunities: Provide opportunities for skill development, training, and learning experiences that challenge individuals to expand their capabilities and knowledge.

Celebrate Effort and Progress: Recognize and celebrate efforts, resilience, and improvements made by individuals or teams. Highlight examples of growth mindset in action to inspire others.

Create a Safe Space for Risk-Taking: Create a safe and supportive environment where individuals feel comfortable taking risks and experimenting with new ideas without fear of failure or criticism.

Encourage Reflection and Self-Assessment: Promote self-reflection and self-assessment practices where individuals can evaluate their own progress, strengths, and areas for growth. Provide tools and guidance for setting meaningful learning goals.

Provide Resources and Support: Offer resources, tools, and mentorship opportunities to support individuals in their learning and development journey. Ensure access to learning materials and opportunities for continuous improvement.

Celebrate Collective Growth: Foster a sense of community and collective growth where individuals support each other's learning and celebrate the achievements of the team or organization as a whole.

By applying these techniques, individuals can actively foster and cultivate a growth-oriented mindset in themselves and others, promoting continuous learning, resilience, and personal development in various aspects of life and work.

4.2 Discuss the role of effort, persistence, and learning from failure in developing a growth mindset

Effort, persistence, and learning from failure are fundamental aspects in developing and cultivating a growth mindset. Here's how each plays a crucial role:

Effort:

Key Concept: A growth mindset emphasizes the belief that abilities and intelligence can be developed through effort and dedication rather than being fixed traits.

Role in Development: Emphasizing the importance of effort encourages individuals to engage in deliberate practice and continuous learning. It shifts the focus from innate talent to the process of improvement and mastery.

Impact: When individuals believe that their effort directly influences their outcomes, they are more likely to persist in the face of challenges and setbacks. This builds resilience and fosters a proactive approach to overcoming obstacles.

Persistence:

Key Concept: Persistence refers to the ability to continue striving towards goals despite difficulties, setbacks, or failures.

Role in Development: Developing a growth mindset involves understanding that setbacks and failures are part of the learning process. Persistence allows individuals to maintain motivation and momentum even when faced with obstacles.

Impact: Persistent individuals view challenges as opportunities to learn and grow rather than reasons to give up. They are more likely to seek alternative strategies, learn from feedback, and adapt their approaches to achieve their goals over time.

Learning from Failure:

Key Concept: Failure is viewed as a temporary setback or a learning opportunity rather than a reflection of one's abilities or potential.

Role in Development: Embracing a growth mindset involves reframing failures as valuable learning experiences. It encourages individuals to analyze what went wrong, identify areas for improvement, and adjust their strategies accordingly.

Impact: Learning from failure fosters resilience and adaptive thinking. It helps individuals develop problem-solving skills, resilience in the face of adversity, and a willingness to take calculated risks in pursuit of personal growth and development.

Integration of Effort, Persistence, and Learning from Failure:

Effort and persistence are closely intertwined with learning from failure in the development of a growth mindset. When individuals consistently apply effort, persevere through challenges, and actively learn from setbacks, they reinforce the belief that their abilities are not fixed but can be developed over time.

This integration promotes a cycle of continuous improvement where challenges are embraced, efforts are sustained, and failures are seen as steppingstones towards achieving greater success. It encourages a proactive and optimistic approach to personal and professional growth, ultimately fostering resilience, adaptability, and a commitment to lifelong learning.

In summary, effort, persistence, and learning from failure are essential components of developing a growth mindset. They enable individuals to view challenges as opportunities, maintain motivation in the face of adversity, and continually strive for improvement and mastery in various aspects of life.

3 More points for each area:

Effort:

Incremental Improvement: A growth mindset encourages individuals to focus on making incremental improvements through consistent effort. Small, consistent steps toward goals reinforce the belief that progress is achievable through sustained dedication.

Embracing Challenges: Effort in a growth mindset involves actively seeking out challenges that stretch current abilities. By embracing challenges, individuals learn to expand their skills and knowledge base, leading to continuous growth.

Effort as a Habit: Developing a growth mindset involves making effort a habitual part of daily routines. By prioritizing effort over immediate results, individuals cultivate resilience and perseverance in pursuit of long-term goals.

Persistence:

Adaptability in Approach: Persistence in a growth mindset entail being adaptable in problem-solving approaches. Individuals learn to adjust strategies based on feedback, setbacks, and changing circumstances, fostering agility and creative thinking.

Goal-oriented Focus: Persistent individuals maintain a strong focus on long-term goals while being flexible in short-term tactics. This dual approach helps in navigating obstacles and staying committed to overarching objectives despite challenges.

Self-regulation: Developing a growth mindset involves cultivating self-regulation skills to manage distractions, setbacks, and emotions. By maintaining emotional balance and a positive outlook, individuals sustain motivation and perseverance over time.

Learning from Failure:

Reflective Practice: Learning from failure in a growth mindset involves engaging in reflective practices. Individuals critically assess their actions, decisions, and outcomes to extract valuable insights and identify areas for improvement.

Resilience Building: Failure in a growth mindset serves as a platform for building resilience. By bouncing back from setbacks stronger and more determined, individuals develop the confidence to face future challenges with optimism and adaptability.

Iterative Problem-solving: Embracing failure as a learning opportunity encourages iterative problem-solving. Individuals experiment with different approaches, learn from mistakes, and refine strategies to achieve better outcomes in subsequent attempts.

These additional points underscore the importance of effort, persistence, and learning from failure in fostering a growth mindset. They highlight how these elements contribute to continuous personal and professional development, resilience, and adaptive learning strategies.

4.3 Offer tips for creating environments and communities that support and encourage growth and development

Creating environments and communities that support and encourage growth and development, especially in fostering a growth mindset, involves cultivating a culture that values learning, collaboration, and continuous improvement. Here are tips for creating such environments:

Promote Psychological Safety: Ensure that individuals feel safe to take risks, share ideas, and ask questions without fear of criticism or judgment. Encourage open communication and constructive feedback.

Set Clear Expectations: Establish clear goals, expectations, and standards for growth and development within the community or organization. Clearly communicate these expectations to align everyone's efforts toward common objectives.

Encourage Lifelong Learning: Foster a culture of continuous learning by providing access to resources, training, workshops, and development programs. Encourage individuals to pursue ongoing education and skill enhancement.

Model Growth Mindset Behaviors: Leaders and influencers within the community should model growth mindset behaviors such as embracing challenges, learning from failures, and seeking feedback. Demonstrate a commitment to personal growth and development.

Celebrate Effort and Progress: Recognize and celebrate efforts, milestones, and improvements made by individuals or teams. Highlight examples of growth mindset in action to inspire others and reinforce desired behaviors.

Facilitate Collaboration: Create opportunities for collaboration, teamwork, and peer learning. Encourage individuals to share knowledge, skills, and experiences to support each other's growth and development.

Provide Mentorship and Coaching: Pair individuals with mentors or coaches who can provide guidance, support, and encouragement in their professional or personal growth journey. Mentorship fosters skill development and confidence.

Encourage Innovation and Creativity: Foster an environment that values innovation and creative thinking. Encourage individuals to explore new ideas, experiment with different approaches, and contribute to continuous improvement initiatives.

Create Feedback Loops: Establish regular feedback mechanisms where individuals receive constructive feedback on their performance, progress, and areas for improvement. Encourage self-reflection and goal setting based on feedback received.

Promote Inclusivity and Diversity: Embrace inclusivity and diversity within the community to foster a range of perspectives, experiences, and ideas. Create opportunities for individuals from diverse backgrounds to contribute and thrive.

Provide Resources and Support: Ensure access to resources, tools, and technology that support growth and development initiatives. Invest in professional development opportunities and support individuals in pursuing their career aspirations.

Monitor and Measure Progress: Track and measure progress towards growth and development goals. Use data and insights to identify areas of strength and improvement, and adjust strategies as needed to support ongoing growth.

By implementing these tips, organizations, educational institutions, and communities can create environments that not only support but actively encourage growth mindset principles. This fosters a culture of continuous improvement, resilience, and achievement among individuals, contributing to overall success and well-being.

Summary for Chapter 4: Cultivating a Growth Mindset

4.1 Explore techniques for fostering a growth-oriented mindset in oneself and others:

Chapter 4 delves into various techniques aimed at fostering a growth-oriented mindset both personally and within a community. It emphasizes the importance of embracing challenges as opportunities for learning and growth. Techniques discussed include setting learning goals, persisting through setbacks, seeking feedback, and practicing self-reflection. The chapter highlights the role of effort and resilience in developing a belief that abilities can be cultivated through dedication and perseverance. It also encourages individuals to challenge fixed mindset beliefs and adopt a proactive approach to personal and professional development.

4.2 Discuss the role of effort, persistence, and learning from failure in developing a growth mindset:

The chapter emphasizes the foundational elements of effort, persistence, and learning from failure in cultivating a growth mindset. Effort is portrayed as essential for skill development and mastery, shifting focus from innate talent to continuous improvement. Persistence is discussed as the ability to maintain motivation and adaptability in the face of challenges, promoting resilience and long-term goal achievement. Learning from failure is presented as a crucial aspect of growth mindset development, encouraging individuals to view setbacks as opportunities for reflection and refinement of strategies.

4.3 Offer tips for creating environments and communities that support and encourage growth and development:

The final section of Chapter 4 provides practical tips for fostering environments and communities that nurture growth mindset principles. It advocates for promoting psychological safety where individuals feel empowered to take risks, share ideas, and receive constructive feedback. Clear expectations and goals are highlighted as essential for aligning efforts towards growth and development. The chapter suggests encouraging lifelong learning through access to resources, mentorship programs, and collaborative opportunities. It stresses the importance of celebrating effort and progress, fostering inclusivity, and providing ongoing support and feedback loops to sustain a culture of growth and development.

In essence, Chapter 4 underscores the significance of intentional practices and environments in fostering a growth mindset. By implementing techniques for personal growth and creating supportive communities, individuals and organizations can cultivate resilience, adaptability, and a commitment to continuous learning and improvement.

"Cultivating a growth mindset is a lifelong endeavor, where every setback becomes a lesson and every effort a step towards greater resilience and success." – Author

Key Takeaways

4.1 Explore techniques for fostering a growth-oriented mindset in oneself and others:

Embrace challenges as opportunities for learning and growth.

Set specific learning goals to focus efforts and measure progress.

Persist through setbacks and view failures as learning experiences.

Seek feedback actively to gain insights and improve performance.

Practice self-reflection to identify strengths, areas for improvement, and growth opportunities.

Challenge fixed mindset beliefs by emphasizing effort and resilience in achieving goals.

4.2 Discuss the role of effort, persistence, and learning from failure in developing a growth mindset:

Effort is foundational for developing skills and achieving mastery.

Persistence enables individuals to maintain motivation and adaptability in the face of challenges.

Learning from failure encourages resilience and adaptive problem-solving.

Viewing setbacks as temporary and surmountable promotes a growth-oriented mindset.

Effort, persistence, and learning from failure collectively reinforce the belief that abilities can be developed through dedication and perseverance.

4.3 Offer tips for creating environments and communities that support and encourage growth and development:

Foster psychological safety where individuals feel comfortable taking risks and sharing ideas.

Set clear expectations and goals to align efforts towards growth and development.

Promote lifelong learning through access to resources, mentorship, and professional development opportunities.

Celebrate effort, progress, and achievements to reinforce growth mindset behaviors.

Create inclusive environments that value diverse perspectives and contributions.

Provide ongoing support, feedback, and opportunities for reflection to sustain a culture of continuous improvement.

These key takeaways highlight actionable strategies and principles that individuals and organizations can adopt to foster a growth mindset. By implementing these practices, individuals can enhance their ability to learn, adapt, and achieve personal and professional goals while contributing to a supportive and growth-oriented community or workplace.

Action Steps

4.1 Explore techniques for fostering a growth-oriented mindset in oneself and others:

Embrace Challenges:

Identify one challenge or goal that stretches your current abilities.

Break down the challenge into smaller, manageable tasks.

Set a timeline for completing each task and monitor progress.

Set Learning Goals:

Define specific, measurable learning goals related to a skill or area of interest.

Create an action plan outlining steps to achieve each goal.

Regularly review and adjust goals based on progress and feedback received.

Persist Through Setbacks:

Reflect on a recent setback or failure and identify lessons learned.

Develop a resilience plan that includes coping strategies for handling setbacks.

Stay committed to your goals by revisiting your motivation and adjusting your approach if necessary.

Seek Feedback Actively:

Identify a mentor, coach, or trusted colleague to provide constructive feedback.

Schedule regular check-ins to discuss progress, challenges, and areas for improvement.

Act on feedback by implementing suggested changes and monitoring their impact.

Practice Self-Reflection:

Dedicate time each week for self-reflection on your growth mindset journey.

Journal about your experiences, insights gained, and areas where you can further develop.

Set aside moments to celebrate your successes and acknowledge your efforts.

Challenge Fixed Mindset Beliefs:

Identify and challenge one fixed mindset belief you hold about your abilities or potential.

Replace it with a growth-oriented perspective by focusing on effort and growth.

Monitor your thoughts and reactions to reinforce your new mindset over time.

4.2 Discuss the role of effort, persistence, and learning from failure in developing a growth mindset:

Effort:

Commit to allocating dedicated time each day or week for skill development.

Practice deliberate practice techniques to improve specific skills or knowledge areas.

Keep a journal to track your efforts and reflect on how they contribute to your growth.

Persistence:

Identify a long-term goal that requires persistence and dedication.

Create a roadmap with milestones to measure progress along the way.

Stay motivated by visualizing success and reminding yourself of the benefits of achieving your goal.

Learning from Failure:

Reflect on a recent failure or setback and analyze what went wrong and what you can learn from it.

Develop a plan for applying lessons learned to future challenges or projects.

Share your experience with others to normalize failure as a part of the learning process.

4.3 Offer tips for creating environments and communities that support and encourage growth and development:

Foster Psychological Safety:

Initiate open discussions about challenges and encourage sharing of diverse perspectives.

Model vulnerability by sharing your own growth experiences and setbacks.

Provide constructive feedback in a supportive manner to promote learning and growth.

Set Clear Expectations:

Communicate organizational or team goals and expectations related to growth and development.

Encourage individuals to align their personal goals with organizational objectives.

Regularly revisit goals and provide updates on progress to maintain clarity and motivation.

Promote Lifelong Learning:

Establish a learning and development budget or fund for employees to pursue training and education.

Offer access to online courses, workshops, or conferences relevant to their roles or interests.

Encourage employees to share new knowledge and skills with their peers to foster a culture of continuous learning.

Celebrate Effort and Progress:

Implement a recognition program that celebrates milestones, efforts, and achievements related to growth mindset behaviors.

Showcase success stories and testimonials from individuals who have demonstrated a commitment to growth and development.

Host regular events or ceremonies to acknowledge contributions and inspire others to embrace a growth mindset.

Create Inclusive Environments:

Implement diversity and inclusion initiatives to ensure all voices are heard and valued.

Encourage collaboration across diverse teams to leverage different perspectives and experiences.

Provide opportunities for cross-cultural learning and understanding to promote empathy and respect within the community.

Provide Ongoing Support and Feedback:

Establish mentorship programs where experienced individuals can guide and support mentees in their growth journey.

Conduct regular performance reviews that include discussions on growth mindset development and goal setting.

Create feedback mechanisms that allow individuals to receive timely and constructive feedback on their progress and areas for improvement.

These action steps are designed to help individuals and organizations actively cultivate a growth mindset by focusing on personal development, resilience, and creating supportive environments conducive to continuous learning and improvement.

In Chapter 4, we explored the art of cultivating a growth mindset—a transformative approach that fosters resilience, adaptability, and continuous learning. We delved into various techniques for nurturing this mindset within ourselves and inspiring it in others, emphasizing the pivotal roles of effort, persistence, and embracing failure as steppingstones to success. Moreover, we provided practical tips for fostering environments and communities that serve as fertile ground for personal and collective growth."

As we venture into Chapter 5, our focus shifts to the profound relationship between mindset and resilience when faced with challenges and setbacks. Here, we examine how individuals with a growth-oriented mindset navigate adversity with unwavering determination and optimism. Through compelling stories and real-life examples, we illustrate how embracing challenges can catalyze personal growth and turn setbacks into opportunities for profound transformation. Furthermore, we equip readers with practical strategies for reframing failure as a powerful catalyst for learning and innovation, ensuring that every obstacle becomes a steppingstone toward greater achievement and fulfillment.

Chapter 5: Embracing Challenges and Failures

"Success is not final, failure is not fatal: it is the courage to continue that counts."

— Winston Churchill

In the context of growth mindset, challenges and failures play a crucial role in personal and professional development. Here are some key points illustrating their importance:

Learning Opportunities: Challenges and failures provide valuable learning experiences. They reveal gaps in knowledge, skills, and strategies, offering a chance to reflect, adapt, and improve. Embracing these experiences fosters a deeper understanding and mastery of subjects or skills.

Resilience Building: Facing challenges and experiencing failures help build resilience. Overcoming difficulties strengthens the ability to bounce back from setbacks, cultivating mental toughness and a positive outlook. This resilience is essential for long-term success and well-being.

Innovative Thinking: Challenges and failures encourage creative problem-solving and innovative thinking. They push individuals to think outside the box, explore new approaches, and develop unique solutions. This creativity is vital for adapting to changing circumstances and achieving breakthroughs.

Persistence and Determination: Dealing with obstacles and setbacks reinforces the importance of persistence and determination. A growth mindset teaches that effort and perseverance are key to overcoming difficulties and achieving goals. This persistence leads to greater accomplishments and a stronger work ethic.

Growth and Development: Challenges and failures are catalysts for growth and development. They provide opportunities to step out of comfort zones, take risks, and push boundaries. Embracing these experiences fosters continuous improvement and self-discovery.

Humility and Adaptability: Experiencing failures promotes humility and adaptability. It reminds individuals that mistakes are part of the learning process and that there is always room for improvement. This humility encourages a willingness to learn from others and adapt to new situations.

Motivation and Engagement: Overcoming challenges and learning from failures can increase motivation and engagement. Achieving success after setbacks reinforces the belief in one's abilities and fuels a desire to continue striving for excellence. This motivation is essential for sustained effort and progress.

Building Confidence: Successfully navigating challenges and recovering from failures builds confidence. It demonstrates that setbacks are temporary and that with effort and resilience, goals can be achieved. This confidence empowers individuals to take on new challenges and pursue their aspirations with determination.

Empathy and Support: Experiencing challenges and failures fosters empathy and a supportive mindset. Understanding the difficulties others face promotes compassion and a willingness to offer support and encouragement. This creates a positive and collaborative environment conducive to growth and development.

Realistic Expectations: Embracing challenges and failures helps set realistic expectations. It teaches that progress is not always linear and that setbacks are a natural part of the journey. This perspective reduces frustration and promotes a balanced and patient approach to achieving goals.

In summary, challenges and failures are integral to developing a growth mindset. They provide opportunities for learning, building resilience, fostering innovation, and enhancing personal and professional growth. By embracing these experiences, individuals can unlock their full potential and achieve lasting success.

5.1 Examine the relationship between mindset and resilience in the face of challenges and setbacks

The science of resilience

It explores how individuals adapt and thrive in the face of adversity, trauma, or significant stress. Here are key aspects of the science of resilience:

Adaptation to Adversity: Resilience involves the ability to bounce back from difficult experiences, setbacks, or trauma. It encompasses psychological, emotional, and behavioral adaptation in response to adversity.

Protective Factors: Researchers study protective factors that contribute to resilience, such as supportive relationships, positive emotions, effective coping strategies, and a sense of purpose or meaning in life. These factors help individuals navigate challenges and maintain psychological well-being.

Psychological Processes: Resilience is supported by various psychological processes, including cognitive flexibility (the ability to adapt thinking and behavior to changing circumstances), optimism (a positive outlook on the future), self-regulation (managing emotions and behaviors), and self-efficacy (belief in one's ability to overcome challenges).

Developmental Perspective: Resilience can be viewed through a developmental lens, examining how resilience develops over the lifespan from childhood through adulthood. Early experiences, such as secure attachment relationships and supportive environments, contribute to the development of resilience skills.

Interventions and Training: The science of resilience informs interventions and training programs designed to enhance resilience in individuals and communities. These programs often focus on building coping skills, fostering social support networks, promoting positive thinking patterns, and encouraging adaptive behaviors in response to stress.

Health and Well-Being: Resilience is associated with better physical health outcomes, improved psychological well-being, and overall life satisfaction. It helps individuals maintain a sense of purpose and optimism, even in challenging circumstances.

Overall, the science of resilience emphasizes the capacity for individuals to recover, adapt, and grow stronger in response to adversity. It underscores the importance of fostering resilience through personal strengths, supportive environments, and effective coping strategies.

The Relationship Between Mindset and Resilience in the Face of Challenges and Setbacks

Understanding the relationship between mindset and resilience is essential for navigating life's inevitable challenges and setbacks. A growth mindset, which is the belief that abilities and intelligence can be developed through dedication and hard work, directly influences one's resilience, or the capacity to recover quickly from difficulties. Here's a detailed examination of how mindset and resilience interact and bolster each other:

1. Growth Mindset Fosters Resilience

A growth mindset encourages individuals to view challenges as opportunities to learn and grow. This perspective is crucial for resilience because it reframes setbacks not as failures, but as valuable experiences that contribute to personal development. When people believe they can improve through effort, they are more likely to persevere in the face of difficulties, thus demonstrating resilience.

2. Resilient Responses to Failure

Individuals with a growth mindset are more likely to respond to failure with a resilient attitude. Instead of feeling defeated or discouraged, they analyze what went wrong, identify lessons learned, and adjust their strategies accordingly. This proactive approach to failure helps them bounce back more quickly and effectively, strengthening their resilience over time.

3. Emotional Regulation and Positive Outlook

A growth mindset helps individuals maintain a positive outlook even during challenging times. This positive outlook is a key component of resilience, as it enables people to manage their emotions, stay motivated, and keep moving forward despite setbacks. By focusing on potential growth and improvement, they can regulate negative emotions and reduce stress, which further enhances their resilience.

4. Effort and Persistence

A central tenet of the growth mindset is the belief in the power of effort and persistence. This belief underpins resilience by encouraging individuals to keep trying, even when progress is slow, or obstacles seem insurmountable. The understanding that persistent effort will eventually lead to improvement motivates individuals to stay committed and resilient in their pursuits.

5. Adaptability and Flexibility

Resilience requires adaptability, the ability to adjust to new circumstances and find alternative solutions when faced with challenges. A growth mindset supports adaptability by fostering a willingness to embrace change, experiment with new approaches, and learn from diverse experiences. This flexibility helps individuals remain resilient in the face of unpredictable and changing environments.

6. Supportive Relationships and Community

A growth mindset also promotes resilience through the cultivation of supportive relationships and a sense of community. Individuals with a growth mindset are more likely to seek feedback, collaborate with others, and build networks of support. These connections provide emotional support, practical advice, and encouragement, all of which are essential for maintaining resilience during difficult times.

7. Long-term Perspective

A growth mindset encourages individuals to take a long-term perspective on their goals and challenges. This perspective helps them stay resilient by reminding them that setbacks are temporary, and that progress is a gradual process. By keeping their focus on long-term growth and improvement, they can maintain motivation and resilience, even when short-term outcomes are disappointing.

In summary, the relationship between mindset and resilience is deeply intertwined. A growth mindset fosters resilience by encouraging a positive outlook, promoting effort and persistence, enhancing adaptability, and supporting the development of strong relationships. By cultivating a growth mindset, individuals can strengthen their resilience, enabling them to navigate challenges and setbacks with greater confidence and effectiveness. This dynamic interplay between mindset and resilience is fundamental for achieving personal and professional success in the face of adversity.

5.2 Share stories of individuals who have turned adversity into opportunity through a growth-oriented mindset

Stories of Individuals Turning Adversity into Opportunity Through a Growth-Oriented Mindset

1. J.K. Rowling: From Rejection to Global Phenomenon

J.K. Rowling, the author of the Harry Potter series, is a prime example of turning adversity into opportunity through a growth mindset. Before her success, Rowling faced numerous rejections from publishers. Living as a single mother on welfare, she continued to believe in her story and her writing abilities. With persistence and determination, she finally secured a publisher, and the Harry Potter series went on to become a global phenomenon. Rowling's resilience and growth mindset turned her initial rejections into a powerful success story, demonstrating the transformative power of perseverance.

2. Thomas Edison: Inventing Through Failure

Thomas Edison, one of history's most prolific inventors, faced countless failures on his way to creating the electric light bulb. Edison famously remarked, "I have not failed. I've just found 10,000 ways that won't work." His growth mindset allowed him to view each failure as a learning opportunity rather than a setback. This relentless pursuit of improvement and innovation eventually led to the successful development of the light bulb, revolutionizing modern life. Edison's story illustrates how a growth mindset can transform repeated failures into the steppingstones of success.

3. Oprah Winfrey: Overcoming Hardship

Oprah Winfrey's rise from a troubled childhood to becoming one of the most influential media personalities in the world is a testament to the power of a growth-oriented mindset. Facing poverty, abuse, and numerous personal challenges, Winfrey used these adversities as fuel for her ambition and resilience. She continually sought to improve herself, learned from her experiences, and embraced new opportunities. Her success in building a media empire and using her platform to inspire millions highlights how a growth mindset can turn even the most difficult circumstances into opportunities for greatness.

4. Nelson Mandela: Transforming Struggle into Leadership

Nelson Mandela's journey from imprisonment to becoming South Africa's first black president exemplifies how a growth mindset can transform personal and national adversity into triumph. During his 27 years in prison, Mandela maintained his belief in justice and equality, using his time to study, reflect, and plan for a better future. His resilience and unwavering commitment to his values enabled him to emerge from prison as a powerful leader who helped dismantle apartheid and unite a divided nation. Mandela's story underscores the importance of a growth mindset in overcoming immense personal and political challenges.

5. Sara Blakely: Embracing Failure in Business

Sara Blakely, the founder of Spanx, transformed her setbacks into a billion-dollar business empire through a growth-oriented mindset. Blakely faced numerous rejections and challenges while developing her first product, but she persisted in refining her idea and pitching it to potential investors. Embracing each failure as a learning experience, she eventually succeeded in creating a product that revolutionized the shapewear industry. Blakely's journey from door-to-door fax machine saleswoman to self-made billionaire demonstrates how resilience and a willingness to learn from failure can lead to extraordinary success.

6. Stephen Hawking: Thriving Despite Disability

Renowned physicist Stephen Hawking's life is a remarkable example of overcoming adversity with a growth mindset. Diagnosed with ALS (amyotrophic lateral sclerosis) at the age of 21 and given only a few years to live, Hawking did not allow his condition to deter him from pursuing his passion for theoretical physics. Despite his physical limitations, he continued to conduct groundbreaking research, write influential books, and inspire millions with his insights into the universe. Hawking's ability to thrive in the face of severe adversity highlights the power of a growth mindset in achieving greatness against all odds.

7. Malala Yousafzai: Advocating for Education

Malala Yousafzai's story of resilience and advocacy for girls' education is a powerful example of turning personal adversity into a global movement. After surviving an assassination attempt by the Taliban for her activism, Malala continued to fight for the right to education for girls worldwide. Her unwavering commitment to her cause, despite the dangers and challenges, earned her the Nobel Peace Prize and global recognition. Malala's growth mindset enabled her to transform her personal struggle into a powerful force for change, inspiring millions to join her in advocating for education and equality.

These stories demonstrate that a growth-oriented mindset can turn adversity into opportunity. By embracing challenges, learning from failures, and persisting in the face of setbacks, individuals can achieve remarkable success and make significant contributions to society. The experiences of J.K. Rowling, Thomas Edison, Oprah Winfrey, Nelson Mandela, Sara Blakely, Stephen Hawking, and Malala Yousafzai illustrate the transformative power of resilience and a growth mindset in overcoming adversity and achieving greatness.

5.3 Provide strategies for reframing failure as a learning experience and fuel for growth

Strategies for Reframing Failure as a Learning Experience and Fuel for Growth

1. Shift Your Perspective

To reframe failure as a learning experience, start by changing your mindset. View failure not as a negative outcome, but as an essential part of the learning process. Understand that failure is a temporary setback and an opportunity to gain valuable insights. Embrace the idea that each failure brings you closer to success by teaching you what doesn't work and highlighting areas for improvement.

2. Analyze and Reflect

After experiencing a failure, take time to analyze what went wrong. Reflect on the steps you took, the decisions you made, and the factors that contributed to the outcome. This introspective approach helps you identify specific mistakes and learn from them. By understanding the root causes of failure, you can develop strategies to avoid similar pitfalls in the future.

3. Embrace a Growth Mindset

Cultivate a growth mindset, which is the belief that abilities and intelligence can be developed through dedication and hard work. Recognize that failure is a natural part of the growth process and an opportunity to improve. Embrace challenges, persist through obstacles, and see effort as a path to mastery. A growth mindset encourages resilience and a proactive approach to learning from failure.

4. Set Realistic Expectations

Set realistic and attainable goals to minimize the fear of failure. Break down larger objectives into smaller, manageable tasks. This approach allows you to experience incremental successes and reduces the impact of setbacks. Realistic expectations help you stay motivated and focused, even when faced with failures, by reinforcing the idea that progress is made step by step.

5. Seek Feedback and Support

Reach out to mentors, colleagues, or peers for feedback and support after experiencing failure. Constructive criticism provides valuable insights and alternative perspectives that can help you learn and grow. Support from others also helps you stay motivated and resilient, reinforcing the idea that failure is a shared experience and an opportunity for collective learning.

6. Document Lessons Learned

Keep a journal or log to document the lessons learned from each failure. Writing down your reflections and insights helps you internalize the learning process and track your progress over time. This practice also provides a reference point for future challenges, reminding you of past experiences and the growth that resulted from them.

7. Focus on the Process, Not Just the Outcome

Shift your focus from solely achieving the end goal to appreciating the process of getting there. Recognize that the journey, with its successes and failures, is where growth occurs. Celebrate the effort, persistence, and learning that happen along the way. By valuing the process, you reduce the fear of failure and increase your resilience in the face of setbacks.

8. Reframe Negative Self-Talk

Challenge and reframe negative self-talk that arises from failure. Replace self-critical thoughts with positive affirmations and constructive self-talk. For example, instead of thinking, "I failed because I'm not good enough," reframe it to, "I didn't succeed this time, but I learned valuable lessons that will help me improve." Positive self-talk fosters a healthier mindset and encourages resilience.

9. Develop Problem-Solving Skills

Enhance your problem-solving skills to better navigate failures. Approach failures with a problem-solving mindset, seeking creative solutions and alternative approaches. By developing these skills, you become more adept at overcoming obstacles and turning failures into opportunities for growth.

10. Cultivate Resilience

Build resilience by practicing self-care, maintaining a positive outlook, and staying connected with supportive people. Resilience helps you bounce back from failures more quickly and with greater strength. Engage in activities that boost your mental and emotional well-being, such as exercise, meditation, and hobbies, to maintain a balanced and resilient mindset.

By implementing these strategies, you can reframe failure as a valuable learning experience and use it as fuel for growth. Embracing failure as a natural part of the journey empowers you to persist through challenges, continuously improve, and ultimately achieve your goals.

Strategies to Cultivate a Resilient Mindset

Resilience being the ability to bounce back from adversity, stress, and challenging situations, developing a resilient mindset can significantly enhance one's capacity to navigate life's ups and downs effectively. Here are several strategies to help cultivate resilience.

1. Embrace a Growth Mindset

A growth mindset, as opposed to a fixed mindset, is the belief that abilities and intelligence can be developed through dedication and hard work.

Continuous Learning: Embrace challenges as opportunities to learn.

Persistence: View setbacks as a natural part of the growth process.

Self-Improvement: Focus on personal development rather than seeking approval from others.

2. Build Strong Relationships

Healthy relationships provide support and encouragement, which are vital for resilience.

Social Connections: Cultivate relationships with family, friends, and colleagues.

Seek Support: Don't hesitate to ask for help when needed.

Empathy and Compassion: Practice kindness and understanding towards others.

3. Develop Emotional Regulation Skills

Managing emotions effectively helps in maintaining a calm and focused mind during adversity.

Mindfulness: Practice mindfulness and meditation to stay present.

Stress Management: Learn techniques such as deep breathing and progressive muscle relaxation.

Positive Reframing: Reframe negative thoughts into positive ones.

4. Set Realistic Goals

Having clear, attainable goals provides direction and purpose.

SMART Goals: Set Specific, Measurable, Achievable, Relevant, and Time-bound goals.

Small Steps: Break down large goals into manageable steps.

Celebrate Achievements: Acknowledge and celebrate progress and accomplishments.

5. Foster Optimism

An optimistic outlook helps in seeing the positives in situations and maintaining hope.

Gratitude Practice: Regularly reflect on things you are grateful for.

Positive Visualization: Imagine positive outcomes and future successes.

Self-Encouragement: Replace self-doubt with self-affirming statements.

6. Strengthen Physical Well-being

Physical health directly impacts mental resilience.

Exercise Regularly: Engage in physical activities that you enjoy.

Healthy Diet: Eat a balanced diet rich in nutrients.

Adequate Sleep: Ensure you get enough restful sleep each night.

7. Develop Problem-Solving Skills

Effective problem-solving abilities enhance confidence in handling challenges.

Identify the Problem: Clearly define the issue at hand.

Brainstorm Solutions: Generate multiple possible solutions.

Evaluate and Act: Choose the best solution and implement it.

8. Maintain a Sense of Purpose

Having a sense of purpose motivates and drives resilience.

Personal Values: Align your actions with your core values.

Meaningful Activities: Engage in activities that give you a sense of fulfillment.

Community Involvement: Participate in community service or volunteer work.

Cultivating a resilient mindset is an ongoing process that involves adopting positive habits, maintaining supportive relationships, and consistently working on personal growth. By implementing these strategies, you can build the mental fortitude needed to navigate life's challenges with confidence and grace.

Summary of Chapter 5: Embracing Challenges and Failures

Chapter 5: Embracing Challenges and Failures - Section Wise Summary

5.1 Examine the Relationship Between Mindset and Resilience in the Face of Challenges and Setbacks

This section delves into how mindset shapes our resilience when confronted with challenges and setbacks. It explores the concept of a fixed mindset versus a growth mindset, highlighting how individuals with a growth mindset view challenges as opportunities for learning and growth. The text explains that a growth mindset fosters resilience by encouraging persistence and adaptability. The relationship between mindset and resilience is illustrated through examples, demonstrating that those who embrace a growth mindset are more likely to bounce back from failures and continue striving toward their goals.

5.2 Share Stories of Individuals Who Have Turned Adversity into Opportunity Through a Growth-Oriented Mindset

In this section, readers are introduced to inspiring stories of individuals who have transformed adversity into opportunity by adopting a growth-oriented mindset. These narratives include historical figures, contemporary leaders, and everyday people who faced significant challenges but used their setbacks as steppingstones to success. Each story emphasizes the pivotal role of mindset in overcoming obstacles, showing how these individuals redefined failure, embraced challenges, and ultimately achieved remarkable outcomes. The section serves as a source of motivation, illustrating the power of a growth mindset in turning adversity into a catalyst for positive change.

5.3 Provide Strategies for Reframing Failure as a Learning Experience and Fuel for Growth

The final section offers practical strategies for reframing failure and using it as a foundation for growth. It presents actionable steps such as shifting perspective to view failure as a learning opportunity, analyzing and reflecting on failures to extract valuable lessons, and embracing a growth mindset to foster resilience. Additional strategies include setting realistic expectations, seeking feedback and support, documenting lessons learned, focusing on the process rather than just the outcome, reframing negative self-talk, developing problem-solving skills, and cultivating resilience. These strategies are designed to help readers change their relationship with failure, turning it into a powerful tool for personal and professional development.

Each section of Chapter 5 provides a comprehensive understanding of how to embrace challenges and failures, illustrating the importance of mindset in navigating setbacks and offering concrete methods for transforming failures into opportunities for growth. This chapter encourages readers to develop resilience, adopt a growth mindset, and view every challenge as a chance to learn and improve.

Key Takeaways

Chapter 5: Embracing Challenges and Failures - Key Takeaways Section Wise

5.1 Examine the Relationship Between Mindset and Resilience in the Face of Challenges and Setbacks

Mindset Shapes Resilience: A growth mindset enhances resilience, encouraging individuals to persist and adapt in the face of challenges.

Growth vs. Fixed Mindset: Those with a growth mindset see challenges as opportunities for learning, while a fixed mindset perceives them as threats.

Examples of Resilience: Illustrations and examples highlight how adopting a growth mindset can lead to better outcomes and a more resilient approach to setbacks.

5.2 Share Stories of Individuals Who Have Turned Adversity into Opportunity Through a Growth-Oriented Mindset

Inspiration from Real-Life Stories: Real-life examples of people who turned adversity into opportunity demonstrate the power of a growth mindset.

Transforming Adversity: The stories show how setbacks can be redefined as steppingstones to success when approached with a growth mindset.

Role Models of Resilience: These narratives serve as motivational role models, proving that overcoming obstacles is possible with the right mindset.

5.3 Provide Strategies for Reframing Failure as a Learning Experience and Fuel for Growth

Perspective Shift: Viewing failure as a learning opportunity rather than a setback is crucial for personal and professional growth.

Action Steps

Practical strategies, such as analyzing failures, setting realistic expectations, and seeking feedback, help reframe failure.

Embrace the Process: Focusing on the process and learning from each experience fosters a growth mindset and builds resilience over time.

Support Systems: Encouraging the use of feedback and support from others to gain new perspectives and insights.

Continuous Improvement: Documenting lessons learned and applying them to future endeavors ensures ongoing personal development.

By understanding these key takeaways, readers can effectively embrace challenges and failures, turning them into valuable opportunities for growth and success. Each section provides insights and strategies to foster a resilient and growth-oriented mindset, empowering individuals to navigate setbacks with confidence and determination.

Transitioning from Chapter 5's exploration of embracing challenges and failure to Chapter 6's focus on nurturing growth in others involves a seamless progression from personal resilience to cultivating environments conducive to collective growth. Chapter 5 delves into the dynamic relationship between mindset and resilience, emphasizing how individuals can leverage challenges and setbacks as catalysts for personal growth. It showcases inspiring stories of individuals who have exemplified a growth-oriented mindset by transforming adversity into opportunities for learning and advancement. These narratives set the stage for Chapter 6, where the discussion shifts to the broader impact of fostering a growth mindset in various spheres of influence.

Chapter 6 shifts its focus to the importance of nurturing growth mindsets in children, students, employees, and team members, recognizing that cultivating such mindsets is foundational to fostering resilience and continuous improvement. It offers practical techniques for leaders and mentors to provide constructive feedback, praise, and encouragement that reinforce a growth-oriented mindset. Moreover, Chapter 6 underscores the pivotal role of leadership in creating environments that support ongoing learning and development, emphasizing the responsibility of leaders to cultivate cultures that prioritize curiosity, experimentation, and adaptation. Together, Chapters 5 and 6 form a cohesive narrative that moves from individual resilience and growth to collective empowerment and organizational excellence, highlighting the transformative power of fostering a growth mindset in both personal and professional settings.

Chapter 6: Nurturing Growth in Others

"Leadership is not about being in charge. It is about taking care of those in your charge."

– Simon Sinek

Nurturing growth in others is a fundamental aspect of personal, professional, and societal development. Here's an illustration of the need for and importance of nurturing growth in others across various contexts:

1. Personal Development

Self-Confidence: Encouraging and supporting someone's growth boosts their self-esteem and confidence. They are more likely to take on new challenges and expand their horizons.

Skill Enhancement: Providing opportunities and guidance for growth helps individuals develop new skills and refine existing ones, leading to personal fulfillment and achievement.

2. Professional Development

Productivity: Employees who feel nurtured and supported are more engaged and productive. They are motivated to contribute positively to the organization.

Innovation: A culture that fosters growth encourages creative thinking and innovation. Employees are more likely to come up with new ideas and solutions.

Leadership: By nurturing growth, organizations cultivate future leaders. Effective leadership development ensures the long-term success and stability of the organization.

3. Societal Development

Economic Growth: Educated and skilled individuals contribute to the economy by filling skilled jobs, starting businesses, and driving innovation.

Social Cohesion: Communities that invest in nurturing growth in their members are more cohesive, with lower crime rates and higher levels of cooperation and trust.

Quality of Life: Societal growth leads to improvements in healthcare, education, and infrastructure, enhancing the overall quality of life.

4. Educational Context

Academic Achievement: Students who receive support and encouragement are more likely to excel academically and pursue higher education.

Lifelong Learning: Encouraging a growth mindset fosters a love for learning that continues throughout life, leading to continual personal and professional development.

5. Relationships

Mutual Respect: Nurturing growth in others builds stronger, more respectful relationships. It shows that you value and care for their development.

Empathy and Understanding: Helping others grow fosters empathy and understanding, creating a more compassionate and supportive environment.

Practical Ways to Nurture Growth

Mentorship and Coaching: Providing guidance and sharing knowledge to help others navigate their personal and professional paths.

Positive Feedback: Offering constructive and positive feedback to encourage progress and development.

Opportunities for Learning: Creating and providing access to learning opportunities, whether through formal education, training programs, or experiential learning.

Supportive Environment: Building an environment that encourages risk-taking, creativity, and personal expression without fear of failure or judgment.

Nurturing growth in others is essential for building a better future, both for individuals and for society as a whole. It creates a ripple effect, where the benefits extend beyond the immediate individual, impacting communities, organizations, and society positively. By investing in the growth of others, we foster a culture of continuous improvement, innovation, and mutual support.

6.1 Discuss the importance of fostering a growth mindset in children, students, employees, and team members

Fostering a growth mindset is crucial in various contexts, including in children, students, employees, and team members. A growth mindset, as defined by psychologist Carol Dweck, is the belief that abilities and intelligence can be developed through dedication and hard work. Here's why it is important to cultivate this mindset across different groups:

1. Children

Resilience: Teaching children a growth mindset helps them develop resilience. They learn to see challenges and failures as opportunities to grow rather than as insurmountable obstacles.

Love of Learning: A growth mindset fosters a love of learning and curiosity. Children become more willing to explore new subjects and activities, enhancing their cognitive and emotional development.

Self-Esteem: Encouraging children to believe in their potential boosts their self-esteem. They become more confident in their abilities and less afraid to take risks or make mistakes.

2. Students

Academic Achievement: Students with a growth mindset are more likely to persist through difficulties, leading to higher academic achievement. They view effort as a path to mastery and are more motivated to work hard.

Adaptability: A growth mindset helps students adapt to new situations and learning environments. They are better equipped to handle the transition from school to college or the workforce.

Problem-Solving Skills: Students learn to approach problems with a can-do attitude, improving their critical thinking and problem-solving skills. They become more innovative and resourceful.

3. Employees

Productivity: Employees with a growth mindset are often more productive. They are motivated to improve their skills and take on new challenges, leading to increased efficiency and output.

Job Satisfaction: Fostering a growth mindset can lead to higher job satisfaction. Employees feel valued and see a clear path for career development, which increases their commitment to the organization.

Collaboration: A growth mindset encourages employees to collaborate and share knowledge. They are more open to feedback and willing to learn from others, fostering a positive and cooperative work environment.

4. Team Members

Innovation: Teams with a growth mindset are more innovative. They are willing to experiment and take risks, which can lead to breakthrough ideas and solutions.

Resilience and Perseverance: Teams that believe in their collective ability to grow and improve are more resilient. They can navigate setbacks and challenges more effectively, maintaining momentum towards their goals.

Positive Culture: A growth mindset contributes to a positive team culture. Team members support each other's development and celebrate successes, creating a supportive and motivating environment.

Practical Strategies for Fostering a Growth Mindset

Modeling Behavior: Leaders, teachers, and parents should model a growth mindset by embracing challenges, showing resilience, and continuously learning.

Praise Effort, Not Just Results: Focus on praising the effort, strategies, and processes that lead to success, rather than just the outcomes. This reinforces the value of hard work and persistence.

Encourage Risk-Taking: Create an environment where taking risks and making mistakes is seen as a natural part of the learning process. Encourage reflection and learning from failures.

Provide Constructive Feedback: Offer feedback that focuses on how to improve and grow. Highlight specific areas for development and provide actionable steps.

Promote Lifelong Learning: Encourage continuous learning and development through professional development opportunities, workshops, and training programs.

Fostering a growth mindset is essential for personal and collective development across various settings. It empowers individuals to embrace challenges, persist through difficulties, and continuously improve. Whether in children, students, employees, or team members, a growth mindset lays the foundation for lifelong learning, innovation, and resilience. By cultivating this mindset, we create environments that support growth, collaboration, and success.

6.2 Offer practical techniques for providing constructive feedback, praise, and encouragement that promote a growth-oriented mindset

Promoting a growth-oriented mindset through constructive feedback, praise, and encouragement involves specific techniques that emphasize effort, improvement, and learning. Here are practical techniques for each:

Constructive Feedback

Be Specific and Actionable

Technique: Focus on specific behaviors or actions that can be improved rather than general comments.

Example: Instead of saying, "Your report is not good," say, "The analysis section of your report lacks depth. Adding more data to support your arguments would strengthen it."

Use the "Feedback Sandwich" Method

Technique: Start with positive feedback, provide constructive criticism in the middle, and end with positive reinforcement.

Example: "Your presentation was engaging and well-organized. To make it even better, try to elaborate more on the financial projections. Overall, your delivery was very confident."

Focus on Effort and Process

Technique: Highlight the effort and strategies used rather than just the outcomes.

Example: "I noticed how much effort you put into researching this topic. Consider organizing your findings into clearer sections to enhance readability."

Encourage Self-Assessment

Technique: Ask questions that encourage individuals to reflect on their performance and identify areas for improvement.

Example: "What part of this project do you feel most confident about, and where do you think you could improve?"

Be Timely and Regular

Technique: Provide feedback as soon as possible after the observed behavior and make it a regular part of communication.

Example: Give immediate feedback after a presentation or performance review instead of waiting for annual evaluations.

Praise

Praise Effort and Persistence

Technique: Acknowledge the hard work and perseverance put into tasks, regardless of the outcome.

Example: "I'm impressed by how persistently you worked on this challenging project. Your dedication is commendable."

Highlight Improvement and Growth

Technique: Recognize progress and development over time.

Example: "You've really improved your writing skills since the last assignment. Your arguments are now much clearer and more compelling."

Be Sincere and Authentic

Technique: Ensure that praise is genuine and specific to the individual's actions.

Example: "Your teamwork on this project was fantastic. Your ability to bring the group together made a significant difference."

Encourage Risk-Taking and Innovation

Technique: Praise attempts at innovative solutions and taking risks, even if they don't always succeed.

Example: "I appreciate how you tried a new approach to solving this problem. It's this kind of thinking that leads to breakthroughs."

Encouragement

Set Realistic Goals and Celebrate Small Wins

Technique: Break larger goals into smaller, achievable steps and celebrate progress along the way.

Example: "Completing the first draft of your thesis is a great milestone. Keep up the good work!"

Use Growth-Oriented Language

Technique: Use language that emphasizes the potential for growth and improvement.

Example: "You haven't mastered this yet, but with continued effort, you will get there."

Provide Opportunities for Development

Technique: Offer opportunities for learning and development, such as workshops, training, and new challenges.

Example: "I think you would benefit from this advanced coding workshop. It will help you develop the skills needed for your next project."

Encourage a Positive Perspective on Challenges

Technique: Frame challenges as opportunities for growth rather than as obstacles.

Example: "This task is tough, but it's a great opportunity to stretch your skills and learn something new."

Be a Role Model

Technique: Demonstrate a growth mindset through your own actions and attitudes.

Example: Share your own experiences of overcoming challenges and learning from mistakes.

By integrating these techniques into your interactions, you can foster a growth-oriented mindset that encourages continuous improvement, resilience, and a love of learning in children, students, employees, and team members.

6.3 Highlight the role of leadership in creating environments that foster continuous learning and development.

Leadership plays a crucial role in creating environments that foster continuous learning and development. Leaders set the tone, establish the culture, and provide the resources and support needed for growth. Here are key aspects of how leadership can promote a culture of continuous learning and development:

1. Leading by Example

Modeling Lifelong Learning: Leaders should demonstrate their own commitment to continuous learning by seeking out new knowledge, skills, and experiences.

Example: A leader who regularly attends workshops, reads industry literature, and pursues advanced degrees inspires their team to value ongoing education.

2. Creating a Learning Culture

Encouraging Curiosity and Innovation: Leaders should foster an environment where curiosity is encouraged, and innovation is celebrated.

Example: Implementing "innovation days" where team members can work on passion projects or explore new ideas can promote a culture of curiosity and experimentation.

Open to Feedback and Improvement: Leaders should cultivate an atmosphere where feedback is welcomed and seen as an opportunity for growth.

Example: Regularly seeking feedback from team members and showing a willingness to make changes based on that feedback sets a powerful example.

3. Providing Resources and Opportunities

Training and Development Programs: Investing in professional development through workshops, courses, and certifications.

Example: Offering access to online learning platforms like Coursera or LinkedIn Learning and encouraging team members to take courses relevant to their roles.

Mentorship and Coaching: Establishing mentorship and coaching programs to support individual growth and development.

Example: Pairing new employees with experienced mentors who can guide them and provide valuable insights into their career paths.

4. Recognizing and Rewarding Growth

Celebrating Achievements: Recognizing and rewarding employees' efforts and achievements in learning and development.

Example: Implementing a rewards system that acknowledges milestones such as completing a challenging project, earning a certification, or contributing innovative ideas.

Promoting from Within: Creating clear pathways for career advancement based on continuous learning and development.

Example: Offering promotions and new opportunities to those who demonstrate a commitment to professional growth and skill acquisition.

5. Encouraging Risk-Taking and Resilience

Creating a Safe Environment for Experimentation: Encouraging employees to take risks and learn from failures without fear of punitive consequences.

Example: Celebrating lessons learned from unsuccessful projects as valuable experiences that contribute to overall growth.

Building Resilience: Supporting team members in developing resilience and a growth mindset by framing challenges as opportunities for development.

Example: Providing training on resilience and stress management techniques and sharing stories of how overcoming obstacles has led to success.

6. Fostering Collaboration and Knowledge Sharing

Encouraging Cross-Functional Teams: Promoting collaboration across different departments to foster knowledge sharing and diverse perspectives.

Example: Organizing regular cross-departmental meetings or team-building activities that encourage employees to share their expertise and learn from one another.

Building Knowledge Repositories: Creating centralized databases or platforms where employees can access and share information, resources, and best practices.

Example: Developing an intranet site with resources such as case studies, training materials, and industry research that employees can utilize and contribute to.

7. Setting Clear Goals and Expectations

Aligning Development with Organizational Goals: Ensuring that individual learning and development goals are aligned with the organization's strategic objectives.

Example: During performance reviews, setting development goals that contribute to both personal growth and the organization's success.

Regular Check-Ins and Progress Reviews: Conducting regular check-ins to monitor progress, provide support, and adjust development plans as needed.

Example: Holding quarterly development meetings to review goals, discuss challenges, and celebrate achievements.

Conclusion

Leadership is instrumental in creating environments that support continuous learning and development. By modeling learning behaviors, fostering a positive learning culture, providing resources, recognizing growth, encouraging risk-taking, promoting collaboration, and setting clear goals, leaders can inspire and enable their teams to achieve continuous personal and professional growth. This not only benefits the individuals but also strengthens the organization, making it more adaptable, innovative, and competitive.

Summary of Chapter 6: Nurturing Growth in Others

6.1 Importance of Fostering a Growth Mindset

Fostering a growth mindset in children, students, employees, and team members is crucial for their long-term development and success. This mindset emphasizes the belief that abilities and intelligence can be developed through dedication and effort, rather than being fixed traits. By promoting a growth mindset:

Children: Encourages resilience in the face of challenges and fosters a love for learning.

Students: Enhances academic performance and prepares them for future challenges.

Employees: Promotes innovation, adaptability, and continuous improvement in the workplace.

Team Members: Builds collaboration and a shared commitment to achieving goals through ongoing learning and skill development.

6.2 Techniques for Promoting a Growth-Oriented Mindset

Practical techniques for providing constructive feedback, praise, and encouragement play a pivotal role in cultivating a growth-oriented mindset:

Constructive Feedback: Focuses on effort, improvement areas, and specific actions to help individuals learn from mistakes and develop skills.

Praise: Acknowledges effort, perseverance, and progress rather than innate abilities, reinforcing the belief that dedication leads to achievement.

Encouragement: Supports individuals in taking on challenges, embracing setbacks as learning opportunities, and maintaining motivation during difficult times.

These techniques create an environment where individuals feel empowered to take risks, learn from failures, and continuously strive for personal and professional growth.

6.3 Leadership's Role in Creating Learning Environments

Leadership plays a critical role in fostering continuous learning and development within organizations:

Setting the Tone: Leaders establish a culture that values learning, growth, and innovation through their words, actions, and priorities.

Providing Resources: Allocating time, funding, and opportunities for training, skill development, and educational programs demonstrates a commitment to employee growth.

Supporting Growth Initiatives: Encouraging mentorship, coaching, and peer learning initiatives fosters collaboration and knowledge-sharing among team members.

Recognizing and Rewarding Growth: Acknowledging and rewarding individuals and teams for their learning achievements and contributions encourages ongoing development and engagement.

By creating an environment where learning is continuous and supported at all levels, leaders empower their teams to adapt to change, drive innovation, and achieve sustainable success.

This summary encapsulates the key insights and strategies from Chapter 6 on nurturing growth in others, emphasizing the importance of fostering a growth mindset, utilizing effective feedback techniques, and leadership's pivotal role in creating environments conducive to continuous learning and development.

"True leadership lies in fostering growth in others, guiding them to see beyond their limits, and inspiring a collective journey towards greatness."

Key Takeaways

6.1 Importance of Fostering a Growth Mindset

Crucial Development: Fostering a growth mindset in children, students, employees, and team members is crucial for their long-term development and success.

Belief in Growth: Emphasize that abilities can be developed through dedication and effort, promoting resilience and a love for learning.

Applications: Applies across various contexts from education to professional settings, enhancing adaptability, innovation, and collaboration.

6.2 Techniques for Promoting a Growth-Oriented Mindset

Constructive Feedback: Focus on effort, improvement areas, and specific actions to support learning and skill development.

Praise and Encouragement: Acknowledge effort, perseverance, and progress to reinforce the belief that dedication leads to achievement.

Environment Creation: Create an environment where individuals feel empowered to take risks, learn from failures, and strive for continuous growth.

6.3 Leadership's Role in Creating Learning Environments

Cultural Influence: Leaders set the tone by establishing a culture that values learning, growth, and innovation.

Resource Allocation: Provide resources such as time, funding, and opportunities for training and development.

Support Mechanisms: Encourage mentorship, coaching, and peer learning to foster collaboration and knowledge-sharing.

Recognition and Reward: Recognize and reward learning achievements to motivate ongoing development and engagement.

These key takeaways highlight the importance of fostering a growth mindset, utilizing effective feedback techniques, and the crucial role of leadership in creating environments conducive to continuous learning and development across different domains.

Action Steps

6.1 Foster a Growth Mindset

Educate and Communicate:

Introduce the concept of growth mindset through workshops, seminars, or discussions.

Provide examples of individuals who have achieved success through perseverance and effort.

Encourage Effort and Persistence:

Emphasize the value of effort over innate talent in achieving goals.

Reward and recognize individuals for their hard work and dedication.

Promote Learning Opportunities:

Offer diverse learning opportunities such as workshops, courses, and skill-building sessions.

Create a culture where mistakes are viewed as learning opportunities rather than failures.

6.2 Techniques for Promoting a Growth-Oriented Mindset

Implement Effective Feedback Mechanisms:

Train managers and leaders in giving constructive feedback that focuses on growth and improvement.

Encourage regular feedback sessions to discuss progress, challenges, and areas for development.

Establish a Culture of Praise and Encouragement:

Encourage peers and supervisors to acknowledge and celebrate efforts and achievements.

Use specific language that highlights progress and improvement rather than fixed traits.

Provide Mentorship and Support:

Pair individuals with mentors who exemplify a growth mindset and can provide guidance.

Foster peer mentoring programs where team members support each other's growth and development.

6.3 Leadership's Role in Creating Learning Environments

Set Clear Expectations and Values:

Clearly communicate organizational values that prioritize continuous learning and growth.

Outline expectations for managers and employees regarding their roles in fostering a learning culture.

Allocate Resources for Learning:

Allocate budget and time for training programs, workshops, and professional development opportunities.

Provide access to online learning platforms and educational resources.

Lead by Example:

Demonstrate a commitment to learning and development through personal participation in training and skill-building activities.

Share personal growth experiences and lessons learned to inspire others.

Establish Feedback Loops:

Implement mechanisms for gathering feedback from employees about their learning experiences and needs.

Use feedback to continuously improve learning initiatives and ensure relevance and effectiveness.

Recognize and Reward Growth:

Develop recognition programs that celebrate milestones, achievements, and contributions to learning.

Tie performance evaluations and rewards to demonstrated growth and skill development.

By implementing these action steps, organizations and leaders can actively nurture a growth mindset, promote effective feedback practices, and create environments that support continuous learning and development among children, students, employees, and team members alike. These steps aim to foster resilience, innovation, and personal fulfillment through ongoing growth opportunities.

Moving from Chapter 6 with focus on nurturing growth in others to Chapter 7 exploration of sustaining personal growth and momentum entails a natural progression from fostering foundational mindsets to applying these principles for long-term development. Chapter 6 emphasizes the critical role of fostering a growth mindset in diverse contexts—whether in children, students, employees, or team members.

It underscores how cultivating this mindset through practical techniques such as constructive feedback and encouragement is essential for fostering resilience and continuous improvement. Moreover, it highlights leadership's pivotal role in shaping environments that prioritize learning and development, setting the stage for individuals and teams to thrive.

Transitioning into Chapter 7, the focus shifts towards sustaining growth and momentum personally. Here, Chapter 7 delves into strategies aimed at maintaining a growth mindset over time, recognizing its significance in achieving enduring success and overcoming challenges. It emphasizes the interconnectedness of self-care, goal-setting, and ongoing learning as foundational pillars that support personal growth and resilience.

Furthermore, Chapter 7 offers practical guidance on navigating obstacles and staying motivated, essential for individuals committed to realizing their full potential. Together, Chapters 6 and 7 provide a comprehensive framework—from nurturing initial mindsets in others to applying these principles for sustained personal growth and achievement, underscoring the journey towards continuous improvement and fulfillment.

Chapter 7: Sustaining Growth and Momentum

"The only limit to our realization of tomorrow is our doubts of today."

— Franklin D. Roosevelt

Sustaining growth and momentum is essential for achieving long-term success and fulfillment, both personally and professionally. The power of mindset, particularly a growth mindset, plays a critical role in maintaining this momentum. Here's why sustaining growth and momentum is important and how mindset influences it:

Need for and Importance of Sustaining Growth and Momentum:

1. Continuous Improvement

Need: In a rapidly changing world, continuous improvement is essential to remain relevant and competitive.

Importance: Sustaining growth ensures that individuals and organizations do not become complacent but instead keep striving for better performance and higher achievements.

2. Adaptability and Resilience

Need: The ability to adapt to new challenges and changing circumstances is crucial in both personal and professional contexts.

Importance: Maintaining momentum in growth helps build resilience, making it easier to navigate setbacks and recover from failures.

3. Long-Term Success

Need: Achieving long-term goals requires consistent effort and progress over time.

Importance: Sustaining growth helps in building a solid foundation for long-term success, whether it's in career development, business growth, or personal achievements.

4. Motivation and Engagement

Need: Without ongoing growth, motivation and engagement can wane, leading to stagnation.

Importance: Continuous growth keeps individuals and teams motivated and engaged, fostering a dynamic and positive environment.

5. Innovation and Creativity

Need: Innovation requires a culture of continuous learning and experimentation.

Importance: Sustaining growth encourages ongoing learning and creativity, leading to innovative solutions and advancements.

Power of Mindset in Sustaining Growth and Momentum

1. Growth Mindset vs. Fixed Mindset

Growth Mindset: Belief that abilities and intelligence can be developed through dedication and hard work.

Impact: Individuals with a growth mindset embrace challenges, persist in the face of setbacks, and see effort as the path to mastery.

Fixed Mindset: Belief that abilities and intelligence are static traits that cannot be significantly developed.

Impact: Individuals with a fixed mindset may avoid challenges, give up easily, and see effort as fruitless if they believe they lack innate talent.

2. Embracing Challenges

Role of Mindset: A growth mindset encourages embracing challenges as opportunities to learn and grow.

Example: Someone with a growth mindset will view a difficult project as a chance to develop new skills and demonstrate resilience.

3. Persistence and Effort

Role of Mindset: A growth mindset fosters persistence and recognizes that sustained effort is necessary for improvement.

Example: An athlete who continually works on their technique and fitness, believing that effort leads to better performance, is demonstrating a growth mindset.

4. Learning from Feedback and Failure

Role of Mindset: A growth mindset involves viewing feedback and failure as valuable information for growth rather than as a negative judgment.

Example: An employee who seeks constructive criticism to improve their performance, rather than feeling discouraged by negative feedback, exemplifies a growth mindset.

5. Adaptability and Flexibility

Role of Mindset: A growth mindset supports adaptability by encouraging openness to new experiences and flexibility in thinking.

Example: A business leader who adapts their strategy in response to market changes, viewing it as a learning opportunity, is using a growth mindset.

Practical Steps to Foster and Sustain a Growth Mindset

Encourage Reflection and Self-Assessment

Regularly reflect on experiences, identify areas for improvement, and celebrate progress.

Example: Keeping a journal of achievements and setbacks to analyze and learn from each experience.

Set Incremental Goals

Break down larger goals into smaller, manageable tasks that provide a sense of achievement and keep momentum going.

Example: Setting weekly or monthly goals that contribute to a larger objective, such as completing a major project or learning a new skill.

Promote a Learning Culture

Foster an environment where continuous learning is valued and supported.

Example: Offering ongoing training programs, encouraging knowledge sharing, and celebrating learning milestones.

Provide Constructive Feedback

Offer specific, actionable feedback that focuses on effort and improvement rather than just outcomes.

Example: In performance reviews, highlight areas of progress and provide guidance on how to further develop skills.

Embrace and Learn from Failure

Normalize failure as part of the learning process and encourage analysis and discussion of what can be learned from it.

Example: Conducting post-mortem reviews after projects to understand what went wrong and how to improve in the future.

Sustaining growth and momentum is vital for long-term success, adaptability, and innovation. A growth mindset plays a crucial role in this process by fostering resilience, encouraging continuous learning, and viewing challenges as opportunities for development. Leaders and individuals alike must cultivate a growth mindset to create environments where continuous growth is not only possible but actively pursued. This mindset shift ensures ongoing progress, motivation, and the ability to thrive in an ever-changing world.

7.1 Explore strategies for maintaining a growth mindset over the long term

Maintaining a growth mindset over the long term requires consistent effort and intentional strategies. 15 effective strategies are stated below with examples to help sustain a growth mindset:

1. Cultivate Self-Awareness

Regular Reflection

Practice: Set aside time regularly to reflect on experiences, achievements, and areas for improvement.

Example: Keep a journal where you document challenges faced, lessons learned, and progress made.

Mindfulness and Meditation

Practice: Engage in mindfulness practices to increase awareness of thoughts and attitudes.

Example: Daily meditation sessions can help in recognizing and redirecting fixed mindset thoughts towards growth-oriented thinking.

2. Set Realistic and Challenging Goals

Incremental Goals

Practice: Break larger goals into smaller, achievable steps to create a sense of progress and achievement.

Example: Instead of setting a goal to become fluent in a new language, set smaller milestones like learning 50 new words each week.

Stretch Goals

Practice: Set ambitious but achievable goals that push you out of your comfort zone.

Example: Challenge yourself to take on a project that requires learning new skills or collaborating with new people.

3. Embrace Challenges and Learn from Failures

Reframe Challenges

Practice: View challenges as opportunities to learn and grow rather than as threats.

Example: When facing a difficult task, remind yourself that it's a chance to develop new skills and build resilience.

Analyze Failures

Practice: Conduct a post-mortem analysis of failures to understand what went wrong and how to improve.

Example: After a project doesn't go as planned, review the process, identify mistakes, and outline steps to avoid them in the future.

4. Foster a Learning Environment

Continuous Learning

Practice: Commit to ongoing education through courses, workshops, and reading.

Example: Enroll in online courses relevant to your field, attend industry conferences, and read books on personal and professional development.

Learning Community

Practice: Surround yourself with people who value growth and learning.

Example: Join professional groups, attend networking events, or participate in online forums where continuous improvement is a shared value.

5. Practice Resilience and Adaptability

Develop Resilience

Practice: Build resilience by practicing stress management techniques and maintaining a positive outlook.

Example: Engage in physical activities, practice gratitude, and maintain a healthy work-life balance to build mental and emotional resilience.

Adapt to Change

Practice: Stay flexible and open to new experiences and changes in plans.

Example: When faced with an unexpected challenge, assess the situation calmly and explore alternative solutions rather than sticking rigidly to the original plan.

6. Seek and Provide Constructive Feedback

Give and Receive Feedback

Practice: Create a culture where feedback is regularly exchanged and seen as a tool for improvement.

Example: During team meetings, encourage open discussions about what went well and what could be improved, and apply this feedback constructively.

Use Feedback Tools

Practice: Utilize tools and frameworks to gather and implement feedback effectively.

Example: Implement 360-degree feedback mechanisms where colleagues, supervisors, and direct reports provide input on performance.

7. Reward Effort and Process, Not Just Outcomes

Recognize Effort

Practice: Focus on recognizing and celebrating the effort and process rather than just the end result.

Example: Acknowledge employees or team members who demonstrate hard work, creativity, and persistence, regardless of the project's final outcome.

Celebrate Milestones

Practice: Celebrate small wins and milestones to keep motivation high.

Example: Host regular team celebrations or personal rewards when key milestones are achieved in the journey towards larger goals.

8. Maintain a Positive Attitude

Positive Self-Talk

Practice: Replace negative self-talk with positive affirmations and growth-oriented statements.

Example: When you catch yourself thinking, "I'm not good at this," reframe it to, "I'm learning and getting better every day."

Gratitude Practice

Practice: Regularly reflect on and express gratitude for the progress made and the opportunities to learn.

Example: Keep a gratitude journal where you write down things you are thankful for each day, focusing on growth experiences.

9. Engage in Lifelong Learning

Diversify Learning Sources

Practice: Explore various sources of knowledge, such as books, podcasts, online courses, and seminars.

Example: Enroll in courses outside your immediate field of expertise to gain new perspectives and skills.

Stay Curious

Practice: Cultivate a habit of asking questions and seeking answers.

Example: When encountering a new concept or idea, take time to research and understand it deeply.

10. Create a Personal Development Plan

Set Long-Term Goals

Practice: Develop a comprehensive plan with long-term goals and periodic reviews.

Example: Outline a five-year career development plan with specific skills to acquire and milestones to achieve.

Regularly Update the Plan

Practice: Revisit and revise the personal development plan based on new insights and changing circumstances.

Example: Adjust your plan quarterly to incorporate new learning opportunities or shifts in career focus.

11. Network with Growth-Oriented Individuals

Join Professional Associations

Practice: Become a member of professional associations and attend their events.

Example: Participate in conferences, webinars, and networking events to connect with like-minded professionals.

Form Accountability Partnerships

Practice: Partner with someone who shares your commitment to growth to keep each other accountable.

Example: Regularly check in with your accountability partner to discuss progress, challenges, and future goals.

12. Embrace Technology and Innovation

Leverage Digital Tools

Practice: Use technology to support your learning and development.

Example: Utilize apps and platforms like Trello for goal tracking, Duolingo for language learning, and Coursera for online courses.

Stay Updated on Technological Trends

Practice: Keep abreast of the latest technological advancements and innovations in your field.

Example: Subscribe to industry newsletters, follow thought leaders on social media, and participate in tech-focused webinars.

13. Develop Emotional Intelligence

Practice Self-Regulation

Practice: Enhance your ability to manage your emotions and reactions in various situations.

Example: Use techniques such as deep breathing, mindfulness, and reflective journaling to stay calm and focused under pressure.

Improve Empathy

Practice: Work on understanding and sharing the feelings of others.

Example: Actively listen to colleagues, ask open-ended questions, and show genuine interest in their perspectives.

14. Cultivate a Problem-Solving Attitude

Focus on Solutions

Practice: Shift your focus from problems to potential solutions and opportunities.

Example: When faced with a challenge, brainstorm multiple solutions and choose the most feasible one to implement.

Practice Critical Thinking

Practice: Enhance your critical thinking skills to analyze situations and make informed decisions.

Example: Regularly engage in activities that require analysis, evaluation, and synthesis, such as puzzles, strategy games, and reading thought-provoking books.

15. Build a Supportive Environment

Create a Growth-Friendly Workspace

Practice: Design a workspace that inspires creativity, productivity, and learning.

Example: Include elements like books, motivational quotes, and comfortable seating in your workspace to create an environment conducive to growth.

Encourage Team Learning

Practice: Foster a culture of shared learning and collaboration within your team or organization.

Example: Implement team learning sessions, where team members present on topics of interest or recent learning experiences.

Maintaining a growth mindset over the long term involves a combination of self-awareness, goal setting, embracing challenges, fostering a learning environment, practicing resilience, seeking feedback, rewarding effort, and maintaining a positive attitude. By consistently applying these strategies, individuals can cultivate and sustain a mindset that values continuous learning and improvement, leading to ongoing personal and professional development.

By engaging in lifelong learning, creating a personal development plan, networking with growth-oriented individuals, embracing technology, developing emotional intelligence, cultivating a problem-solving attitude, and building a supportive environment, individuals can continue to foster and sustain a mindset that values continuous improvement and learning. These strategies will help ensure ongoing personal and professional development, leading to greater fulfillment and success.

7.2 Discuss the importance of self-care, goal-setting, and ongoing learning in sustaining personal growth and resilience

Sustaining personal growth and resilience requires a balanced approach that includes self-care, goal-setting, and ongoing learning. Each of these components plays a critical role in maintaining overall well-being and continuous improvement. Here's why each is important and how they interrelate:

1. Importance of Self-Care

Physical Health

Vitality and Energy: Physical health provides the energy and vitality needed to pursue personal and professional goals.

Example: Regular exercise, a balanced diet, and adequate sleep improve physical health, which enhances focus and productivity.

Mental Health

Stress Management: Self-care practices help manage stress and prevent burnout, which is essential for long-term resilience.

Example: Activities such as meditation, mindfulness, and hobbies help reduce stress and promote mental well-being.

Emotional Well-Being

Emotional Stability: Taking time for self-care helps maintain emotional stability, allowing individuals to better handle challenges and setbacks.

Example: Practicing gratitude, connecting with loved ones, and engaging in activities that bring joy contribute to emotional well-being.

2. Importance of Goal setting

Direction and Focus

Clear Path: Setting goals provides direction and focus, making it easier to channel efforts towards meaningful outcomes.

Example: Setting specific, measurable, achievable, relevant, and time-bound (SMART) goals helps clarify what needs to be done and by when.

Motivation and Engagement

Increased Motivation: Goals serve as motivators, providing a sense of purpose and drive.

Example: Achieving smaller milestones on the way to a larger goal boosts confidence and keeps motivation high.

Measurement and Accountability

Tracking Progress: Goals allow for tracking progress and holding oneself accountable, which is crucial for continuous improvement.

Example: Regularly reviewing and adjusting goals based on progress helps maintain momentum and ensures alignment with overall aspirations.

3. Importance of Ongoing Learning

Skill Development

Enhancing Competence: Ongoing learning ensures continuous skill development, keeping individuals competitive and competent in their fields.

Example: Taking courses, attending workshops, and reading industry literature help keep skills up to date.

Adaptability

Flexibility: Continuous learning fosters adaptability, enabling individuals to respond effectively to changes and new challenges.

Example: Learning new technologies or methodologies helps adapt to evolving job requirements or market conditions.

Personal Fulfillment

Satisfaction and Growth: Lifelong learning contributes to personal fulfillment and intellectual growth, enriching life experiences.

Example: Exploring new hobbies, learning new languages, or studying different cultures broadens perspectives and adds to personal satisfaction.

Interrelationship Between Self-Care, Goal-Setting, and Ongoing Learning

Synergy and Balance

Holistic Growth: Self-care, goal-setting, and ongoing learning work synergistically to support holistic personal growth and resilience.

Example: Practicing self-care ensures you have the energy to pursue your goals, while setting goals provides direction for your learning efforts.

Sustainable Progress

Preventing Burnout: Balancing self-care with goal setting and learning prevents burnout and promotes sustainable progress.

Example: Integrating relaxation and downtime into your schedule ensures you can maintain long-term focus and productivity.

Continuous Improvement

Feedback Loop: Ongoing learning informs goal setting, while achieving goals and practicing self-care provide feedback for further learning and growth.

Example: Reflecting on what you've learned and achieved helps set more informed and effective goals, which in turn guide future learning efforts.

Practical Tips for Integration

Self-Care Routine

Schedule Regular Breaks: Incorporate short breaks throughout the day to recharge.

Exercise and Nutrition: Maintain a regular exercise routine and eat a balanced diet.

Mental Health: Practice mindfulness or meditation regularly.

Effective Goal setting

SMART Goals: Set specific, measurable, achievable, relevant, and time-bound goals.

Review and Adjust: Regularly review progress and adjust goals as needed.

Celebrate Milestones: Acknowledge and celebrate small achievements along the way.

Commitment to Learning

Lifelong Learning Plan: Create a plan that includes both formal and informal learning opportunities.

Stay Curious: Cultivate curiosity by exploring new topics and interests.

Engage with Communities: Join professional groups, attend seminars, and participate in online forums.

Self-care, goal-setting, and ongoing learning are fundamental pillars of sustaining personal growth and resilience. Self-care ensures physical, mental, and emotional well-being, providing the foundation for sustained effort. Goal setting offers direction, motivation, and a framework for measuring progress. Ongoing learning keeps skills relevant, fosters adaptability, and contributes to personal fulfillment. Together, these elements create a balanced approach to continuous improvement, helping individuals thrive in both their personal and professional lives.

7.3 Provide guidance on overcoming obstacles and staying motivated on the journey to realizing one's full potential

Overcoming obstacles and staying motivated on the journey to realizing one's full potential requires a combination of mindset, strategies, and practical actions. Here's a comprehensive guide to help navigate this journey:

1. Cultivating a Resilient Mindset

Embrace a Growth Mindset

Focus on Learning: View challenges and setbacks as opportunities to learn and grow.

Example: When facing a difficult task, remind yourself that effort and perseverance will lead to improvement.

Practice Self-Compassion

Be Kind to Yourself: Treat yourself with the same kindness and understanding you would offer a friend.

Example: Acknowledge your efforts and progress, even if outcomes aren't perfect.

Stay Positive

Maintain Optimism: Focus on positive outcomes and possibilities, rather than dwelling on negative aspects.

Example: Keep a gratitude journal to regularly reflect on and appreciate the good things in your life.

2. Setting Clear and Realistic Goals

Break Down Goals

Incremental Steps: Divide larger goals into smaller, manageable tasks to avoid feeling overwhelmed.

Example: If your goal is to write a book, set milestones for outlining, drafting chapters, and revising.

Prioritize Goals

Focus on Priorities: Determine which goals are most important and tackle those first.

Example: Use the Eisenhower Matrix to prioritize tasks based on their urgency and importance.

SMART Goals

Specific, Measurable, Achievable, Relevant, Time-Bound: Ensure your goals meet these criteria for clarity and feasibility.

Example: Instead of "get fit," set a goal to "exercise for 30 minutes, three times a week for the next three months."

3. Developing Effective Strategies

Create a Plan

Detailed Roadmap: Outline the steps needed to achieve your goals, including resources and timelines.

Example: Use a project management tool like Trello or Asana to organize and track your tasks.

Seek Support

Build a Support Network: Surround yourself with people who encourage and support your growth.

Example: Join a study group, find a mentor, or participate in online forums related to your goals.

Stay Organized

Efficient Systems: Implement organizational systems to manage your time and tasks effectively.

Example: Use calendars, to-do lists, and productivity apps to keep track of your commitments and deadlines.

4. Overcoming Obstacles

Identify and Address Barriers

Analyze Challenges: Identify the specific obstacles you face and develop strategies to address them.

Example: If procrastination is an issue, break tasks into smaller parts and set short deadlines for each part.

Build Resilience

Strengthen Coping Skills: Develop techniques to manage stress and bounce back from setbacks.

Example: Practice mindfulness, exercise regularly, and maintain a balanced lifestyle to enhance resilience.

Problem-Solving Approach

Be Solution-Oriented: Focus on finding solutions rather than getting stuck on problems.

Example: When encountering a roadblock, brainstorm multiple solutions and choose the best one to implement.

5. Staying Motivated

Celebrate Small Wins

Acknowledge Progress: Recognize and celebrate small achievements along the way to maintain motivation.

Example: Treat yourself to something enjoyable after completing a milestone, like watching a favorite movie.

Visualize Success

Positive Visualization: Regularly visualize achieving your goals to stay motivated and focused.

Example: Spend a few minutes each day imagining yourself successfully completing your goals and experiencing the benefits.

Stay Inspired

Find Inspiration: Surround yourself with sources of inspiration, such as books, quotes, and role models.

Example: Read biographies of people you admire or follow motivational speakers on social media.

Maintain Passion and Purpose

Connect with Your Why: Remind yourself of the deeper reasons behind your goals and the impact they will have on your life.

Example: Create a vision board that represents your goals and the reasons behind them and place it where you can see it daily.

6. Continuous Learning and Adaptation

Lifelong Learning

Commit to Growth: Always be open to learning new skills and acquiring knowledge.

Example: Take online courses, attend workshops, and read books related to your goals.

Adapt and Adjust

Stay Flexible: Be willing to adapt your plans and goals as needed based on new information and changing circumstances.

Example: If a particular strategy isn't working, be open to trying different approaches or modifying your goals.

7. Leveraging Resources

Use Available Tools

Technology and Resources: Leverage tools and resources that can help you achieve your goals more efficiently.

Example: Use apps for productivity, language learning, or skill development to support your growth.

Professional Help

Seek Expertise: Don't hesitate to seek professional help when needed, such as coaches, therapists, or consultants.

Example: If you're struggling with time management, a productivity coach can provide personalized strategies and support.

Overcoming obstacles and staying motivated on the journey to realizing one's full potential involves cultivating a resilient mindset, setting clear goals, developing effective strategies, and continuously adapting and learning. By embracing self-compassion, maintaining a positive outlook, and leveraging support systems and resources, individuals can navigate challenges, sustain motivation, and achieve long-term growth and success.

"Sustaining growth requires a relentless pursuit of learning, a commitment to self-care, and the courage to stay the course, even when the path is unclear." – Author

Summary of Chapter 7: Sustaining Growth and Momentum

7.1 Strategies for Maintaining a Growth Mindset Over the Long Term

Continuous Learning: Emphasizes the importance of seeking new challenges and opportunities to learn and grow continuously.

Resilience Building: Discusses strategies for bouncing back from setbacks and maintaining optimism in the face of challenges.

Adaptability: Highlights the need to embrace change and adapt to new circumstances to sustain growth mindset over time.

7.2 Importance of Self-Care, Goal-Setting, and Ongoing Learning

Self-Care: Stresses the significance of prioritizing physical, mental, and emotional well-being to sustain personal growth and resilience.

Goal setting: Discusses effective goal-setting techniques such as SMART goals to maintain focus and motivation.

Ongoing Learning: Emphasizes the role of continuous education and skill development in staying relevant and achieving long-term goals.

7.3 Guidance on Overcoming Obstacles and Staying Motivated

Mindset Shifts: Provides strategies for shifting from a fixed mindset to a growth mindset to overcome self-imposed limitations.

Persistence and Perseverance: Discusses the importance of persistence in the face of challenges and setbacks on the journey to realizing one's full potential.

Motivational Techniques: Offers practical guidance on staying motivated through visualization, affirmations, and surrounding oneself with supportive networks.

This summary encapsulates the key insights and strategies from Chapter 7 on sustaining growth and momentum, focusing on maintaining a growth mindset, practicing self-care and goal setting, and overcoming obstacles to achieve personal and professional growth.

Key Takeaways

7.1 Strategies for Maintaining a Growth Mindset Over the Long Term

Continuous Learning:

Keep challenging yourself with new experiences and learning opportunities.

Embrace setbacks as opportunities for growth and learning.

Resilience Building:

Develop resilience by maintaining optimism and bouncing back from setbacks.

Cultivate a positive attitude and adaptability in the face of change.

Adaptability:

Stay flexible and open to new ideas and approaches.

Embrace change as a natural part of growth and development.

7.2 Importance of Self-Care, Goal-Setting, and Ongoing Learning

Self-Care:

Prioritize self-care to maintain physical, mental, and emotional well-being.

Take breaks, practice mindfulness, and engage in activities that recharge you.

Goal setting:

Set SMART goals (Specific, Measurable, Achievable, Relevant, Time-bound) to stay focused and motivated.

Regularly review and adjust goals based on progress and changing circumstances.

Ongoing Learning:

Commit to lifelong learning to stay relevant and expand your skills.

Seek opportunities for professional development and personal growth.

7.3 Guidance on Overcoming Obstacles and Staying Motivated

Mindset Shifts:

Foster a growth mindset by challenging fixed beliefs and embracing challenges as opportunities.

Practice self-awareness and positive self-talk to overcome limiting beliefs.

Persistence and Perseverance:

Stay committed to your goals and persevere through setbacks.

Celebrate small victories and learn from failures to keep moving forward.

Motivational Techniques:

Use visualization techniques to envision success and stay motivated.

Surround yourself with supportive relationships and networks that encourage growth and resilience.

These key takeaways provide actionable insights into maintaining a growth mindset, practicing self-care and goal setting, and overcoming obstacles to sustain personal growth and momentum over the long term. They emphasize resilience, adaptability, and continuous learning as essential elements in achieving and maintaining success.

Action Steps

7.1 Strategies for Maintaining a Growth Mindset Over the Long Term

Continuous Learning:

Action Steps:

Commit to learning something new regularly, whether through courses, reading, or practical experiences.

Set aside dedicated time each week for reflection on lessons learned and how they contribute to personal growth.

Resilience Building:

Action Steps:

Practice mindfulness and meditation to cultivate resilience and manage stress.

Develop a habit of reframing setbacks as learning opportunities rather than failures.

Adaptability:

Action Steps:

Seek feedback from others on how you can adapt and improve in various aspects of your life.

Embrace change by actively seeking out new challenges or opportunities that stretch your abilities.

7.2 Importance of Self-Care, Goal-Setting, and Ongoing Learning

Self-Care:

Action Steps:

Create a self-care routine that includes activities such as exercise, adequate sleep, and hobbies.

Learn to recognize signs of burnout and implement strategies to recharge and rejuvenate.

Goal setting:

Action Steps:

Set SMART goals that are specific, measurable, achievable, relevant, and time bound.

Break down larger goals into smaller, manageable tasks and create a timeline for completion.

Ongoing Learning:

Action Steps:

Identify areas where you want to grow personally and professionally.

Invest in courses, workshops, or mentorship programs that align with your learning goals and interests.

7.3 Guidance on Overcoming Obstacles and Staying Motivated

Mindset Shifts:

Action Steps:

Challenge negative self-talk and replace it with affirmations that promote growth and resilience.

Seek out role models or mentors who exemplify a positive mindset and learn from their experiences.

Persistence and Perseverance:

Action Steps:

Develop a support network of friends, family, or colleagues who can provide encouragement and accountability.

Celebrate milestones and successes, no matter how small, to maintain motivation and momentum.

Motivational Techniques:

Action Steps:

Practice visualization exercises to imagine achieving your goals and visualize the steps to get there.

Engage in activities that inspire and energize you, whether it's reading motivational books or attending inspiring events.

These action steps are designed to help you implement the principles discussed in Chapter 7, focusing on sustaining a growth mindset, prioritizing self-care and goal setting, and overcoming obstacles to achieve personal growth and resilience over the long term. By taking consistent action and incorporating these practices into your daily routine, you can foster lasting positive change and maintain momentum in your journey toward realizing your full potential.

Conclusion

Reflecting on the journey we have embarked upon together through the exploration of mindset, it is evident how profound an impact our perspectives can have on our lives. From understanding the nuances between fixed and growth mindsets to embracing challenges as opportunities for growth, we've delved deep into the transformative power of intentional thinking. This journey has not only equipped us with valuable insights but also empowered us to navigate life with renewed clarity and purpose.

Throughout this book, we've emphasized the importance of cultivating a growth-oriented mindset. This mindset isn't just about embracing change; it's about actively seeking opportunities to learn, adapt, and evolve. By fostering curiosity and a hunger for knowledge, we've laid the foundation for continuous personal development. As readers, you've embarked on a journey of self-discovery, uncovering your potential to achieve greater heights in all aspects of life.

Applying the principles of mindset isn't confined to theory; it's about practical application in everyday situations. From personal relationships to professional endeavors, the strategies discussed here empower you to approach challenges with resilience and optimism. By reframing setbacks as steppingstones to success and learning from failures, you're poised to navigate obstacles with newfound confidence and determination.

Central to our exploration has been the recognition that setbacks and challenges are inevitable. However, it's our response to these challenges that defines our growth. By embracing a growth mindset, you've cultivated the ability to persevere through adversity, emerging stronger and more resilient. Each setback becomes an opportunity for introspection and improvement, guiding you towards achieving your aspirations with steadfast resolve.

The stories shared throughout this book illustrate the transformative power of mindset in real-life contexts. From individuals who have overcome daunting odds to achieve their dreams to leaders who have fostered environments of innovation and growth, these narratives serve as inspiration for your own journey. By internalizing these stories and drawing lessons from them, you're empowered to chart a course towards personal and professional fulfillment.

Looking ahead, the journey of mindset exploration continues beyond these pages. As you conclude this book, I encourage you to reflect on how these insights can shape your future endeavors. Set meaningful goals, cultivate positive habits, and surround yourself with supportive communities that nurture your growth. Remember, the power of mindset lies not only in what you've learned but in how you apply these principles to create a life of purpose, resilience, and fulfillment.

"Embrace the power of your mindset, for it is the compass that will guide you to the realization of your dreams and the fulfillment of your potential." - Author

Summarize key insights and takeaways from the book.

Mindset Matters: Understanding the difference between fixed and growth mindsets is crucial. A growth mindset fosters resilience, adaptability, and a willingness to learn from setbacks.

Personal Empowerment: By embracing a growth-oriented mindset, individuals can break free from self-limiting beliefs and achieve personal and professional success.

Continuous Learning: Cultivating curiosity and a thirst for knowledge is essential for ongoing personal development. Lifelong learning fosters creativity, innovation, and adaptability.

Overcoming Challenges: Setbacks are opportunities for growth. A growth mindset enables individuals to view challenges as learning experiences and to persevere in the face of adversity.

Positive Habits: Adopting positive habits such as goal setting, self-reflection, and seeking feedback supports the development of a growth mindset and enhances personal effectiveness.

Building Resilience: Resilience is cultivated through the practice of resilience-building techniques like mindfulness, gratitude, and embracing failures as learning opportunities.

Creating Supportive Environments: Surrounding oneself with supportive communities and environments that encourage growth and development reinforces a growth mindset.

Leadership and Influence: Leaders play a crucial role in fostering growth mindsets within teams and organizations. Effective leadership inspires innovation, collaboration, and continuous improvement.

Impact of Mindset on Success: Mindset shapes outcomes in various aspects of life, influencing relationships, career trajectories, and overall well-being.

Ultimately, the power of mindset lies in its ability to transform perspectives and behaviors, enabling individuals to achieve their full potential and lead fulfilling lives.

These insights collectively highlight the transformative potential of mindset in shaping personal growth, resilience, and success. The book encourages readers to adopt a growth-oriented mindset and provides practical strategies for applying these principles in everyday life.

Encouraging readers to embrace the power of mindset in pursuing their dreams.

Embracing the power of mindset can profoundly shape your life and propel you towards achieving your dreams. By adopting a growth-oriented mindset, you unlock a world of possibilities where challenges become opportunities and setbacks become steppingstones to success.

Imagine approaching each day with a mindset that welcomes growth and learning. Rather than seeing obstacles as insurmountable barriers, you view them as chances to learn, adapt, and evolve. This shift in perspective empowers you to tackle challenges with resilience and creativity, paving the way for personal and professional growth.

Moreover, cultivating a growth mindset isn't just about achieving immediate goals; it's about fostering a mindset that supports lifelong learning and continuous improvement. It's about developing the habits and attitudes that sustain your journey towards greatness, whether in your career, relationships, or personal endeavors.

As you embark on this journey of mindset exploration, remember that your beliefs and attitudes shape your reality. By harnessing the power of mindset, you take control of your narrative, turning aspirations into achievements and dreams into tangible realities.

So, I invite you to embrace the power of mindset with an open heart and a curious mind. Explore the insights shared in this book, apply them to your life, and witness the transformative impact firsthand. Together, let's strive towards a future where growth, resilience, and fulfillment define our path to success.

Core message reinforcement!

At its core, the message of embracing the power of mindset is about understanding that your beliefs and attitudes fundamentally shape your experiences and outcomes in life. By cultivating a growth-oriented mindset, you not only open yourself to new possibilities but also equip yourself with the resilience and determination needed to navigate challenges effectively.

This book reinforces the idea that mindset is not just a passive trait but a powerful tool that can be intentionally developed and strengthened. It encourages readers to challenge self-limiting beliefs, embrace failures as learning opportunities, and persist in the face of adversity.

Ultimately, the core message emphasizes that success and fulfillment are within reach for those who cultivate a mindset of growth and possibility. By adopting this mindset, you empower yourself to shape your reality, overcome obstacles, and achieve your goals with confidence and purpose.

Reflection and future perspectives

Reflection and future perspectives on the power of mindset invite us to look back on our journey of growth and consider the lessons learned along the way. It's a moment to pause, acknowledge our progress, and reflect on how our mindset has influenced our achievements and experiences.

Looking back, we might recognize times when a fixed mindset held us back, causing us to doubt our abilities or fear failure. Conversely, moments where we embraced a growth mindset likely brought about breakthroughs, resilience in adversity, and a deeper sense of personal fulfillment.

As we gaze forward, the future beckons with endless possibilities. Cultivating a growth mindset isn't just a one-time endeavor but an ongoing practice that evolves with us. It's about continuing to learn, adapt, and stretch beyond our comfort zones to achieve new heights of success and happiness.

In the realm of personal development, future perspectives urge us to envision the kind of person we aspire to become. Whether in our careers, relationships, or personal pursuits, a growth mindset propels us forward by fostering innovation, courage, and a relentless pursuit of excellence.

Looking ahead, let's commit to nurturing our mindset like a garden—tending to it with care, feeding it with positivity, and pruning away negativity. By doing so, we pave the way for a future filled with resilience, achievement, and the unwavering belief that our potential is limitless.

In conclusion, reflection on our journey with mindset offers profound insights into how far we've come and what lies ahead. Embrace this reflection as a catalyst for future growth, knowing that with the right mindset, every challenge becomes an opportunity, and every dream becomes attainable.

The path ahead - opportunities and challenges

The path ahead is filled with both opportunities and challenges, each presenting a unique opportunity for growth and discovery. As we navigate this journey, it's essential to approach these opportunities with a growth-oriented mindset, ready to learn, adapt, and seize the possibilities that lie before us.

Opportunities abound for those who embrace a growth mindset. It's about seeing potential where others see obstacles and turning challenges into steppingstones for personal and professional development. By cultivating curiosity and resilience, we can explore new avenues, innovate, and make meaningful contributions to our communities and beyond.

However, alongside these opportunities come challenges that test our resolve and commitment to growth. These challenges may include setbacks, uncertainty, or the fear of failure. Yet, with a growth mindset, we view these challenges as essential parts of our journey—opportunities to learn valuable lessons, build resilience, and emerge stronger than before.

To navigate the path ahead effectively, it's crucial to maintain a balanced perspective. Embrace change as a constant companion, recognizing that every experience, whether positive or challenging, contributes to our growth. By staying adaptable and open-minded, we can turn challenges into catalysts for personal transformation and achievement.

In essence, the path ahead is a dynamic interplay of opportunities and challenges, each offering a chance to deepen our understanding of ourselves and the world around us. With a growth mindset as our compass, we can embrace the journey ahead with optimism, courage, and a steadfast determination to realize our fullest potential.

Inspiration and momentum

Inspiration and momentum are twin forces that propel us forward on our journey of growth and achievement. They ignite the spark of creativity, fuel our ambitions, and sustain our momentum even in the face of adversity.

Inspiration often strikes unexpectedly, arising from moments of clarity, connection, or insight. It's a catalyst that sparks ideas, fuels passion, and drives us to pursue our dreams with unwavering determination. By nurturing inspiration through exposure to diverse experiences, learning from others' journeys, and cultivating a curious mindset, we invite creativity to flourish and empower ourselves to innovate and create.

Momentum, on the other hand, is the steady force that keeps us moving forward. It's built through consistent effort, dedication, and resilience in the pursuit of our goals. When we harness momentum, even small steps forward can lead to significant progress over time. By setting achievable milestones, staying focused on our priorities, and celebrating each accomplishment, we maintain the momentum needed to sustain long-term success.

Together, inspiration and momentum form a powerful synergy. Inspiration fuels the initial spark of ideas and aspirations, while momentum provides the sustained energy to turn those aspirations into reality. This dynamic interplay fosters a cycle of continuous growth and achievement, where each success builds upon the last, driving us closer to our vision of success.

In our journey forward, let us cultivate inspiration by seeking out new experiences, learning from diverse perspectives, and staying open to creative possibilities. Let us harness momentum by committing to consistent action, staying resilient in the face of challenges, and maintaining a positive outlook on our progress.

With inspiration as our guide and momentum as our fuel, we are empowered to overcome obstacles, embrace opportunities, and chart a course toward a future filled with fulfillment, purpose, and achievement.

Outcome of the Book

The outcome of the book is multifaceted, aimed at empowering readers to harness the transformative power of mindset in their lives. Through a deep exploration of mindset theory, practical strategies, and inspiring anecdotes, readers are equipped with the tools to:

Develop a Growth-Oriented Mindset: Understand the distinction between fixed and growth mindsets and learn how to cultivate a mindset that embraces challenges, learns from failures, and seeks continuous improvement.

Overcome Self-Limiting Beliefs: Identify and challenge self-limiting beliefs that hinder personal growth and success. Through practical exercises and self-reflection, readers gain insights into reframing negative thoughts and building self-confidence.

Embrace Resilience and Adaptability: Explore how resilience and adaptability are nurtured through a growth mindset. Stories of individuals who have overcome adversity illustrate how setbacks can be transformed into opportunities for growth and personal development.

Navigate Challenges and Failure: Learn strategies for reframing failure as a learning experience and a steppingstone to success. The book provides actionable insights on bouncing back stronger from setbacks and using setbacks as fuel for growth.

Foster Growth in Others: Understand the role of leadership and mentorship in fostering a growth mindset in children, students, employees, and team members. Practical techniques for providing constructive feedback and creating supportive environments are highlighted.

Sustain Personal Growth and Momentum: Gain strategies for maintaining a growth mindset over the long term. From goal setting and self-care to continuous learning and adaptation, readers are empowered to sustain personal growth and momentum throughout their lives.

Inspire Positive Change: Ultimately, the book aims to inspire readers to take proactive steps towards realizing their full potential. By embracing intentional thinking, adopting a growth mindset, and leveraging their strengths, readers are encouraged to create positive change in their lives and communities.

Through these outcomes, the book serves as a comprehensive guide for individuals seeking to unlock their innate potential, overcome challenges, and achieve personal and professional success. It encourages readers to embrace the power of mindset as a fundamental tool for shaping their destinies and pursuing their dreams with confidence and resilience.

The benefits of the book to students, researchers, teachers, managers and leaders and social opinion leaders:

The book "Power of Mindset" offers valuable insights and practical strategies that cater to a diverse audience, including students, researchers, teachers, managers, leaders, and social opinion leaders:

Students:

Mindset Development: Students can learn to cultivate a growth mindset, which enhances resilience, adaptability, and motivation in academic settings.

Overcoming Challenges: Strategies for reframing failure and navigating academic challenges empower students to approach learning with a positive and proactive mindset.

Goal Setting: Techniques for goal setting and sustaining momentum help students achieve academic and personal aspirations effectively.

Researchers:

Mindset Theory: Researchers gain a deeper understanding of mindset theory and its implications for individual development and achievement.

Application in Research: Insights into resilience and adaptability fostered by a growth mindset can inform research on human behavior, learning, and motivation.

Personal Development: Practical exercises for overcoming self-limiting beliefs and sustaining growth provide researchers with tools for personal and professional development.

Teachers:

Classroom Strategies: Teachers can implement strategies for fostering a growth mindset in their students, promoting a culture of resilience and continuous improvement.

Effective Feedback: Techniques for providing constructive feedback and encouragement support teachers in nurturing students' self-confidence and motivation.

Professional Growth: The book offers resources for teachers to enhance their teaching practices and personal growth through mindset development.

Managers and Leaders:

Leadership Development: Managers and leaders learn how to create environments that support growth and innovation, fostering a motivated and resilient workforce.

Decision-Making: Strategies for overcoming challenges and learning from failures enhance leaders' decision-making capabilities and strategic thinking.

Team Development: Techniques for promoting a growth mindset among team members facilitate collaboration, creativity, and high-performance outcomes.

Social Opinion Leaders:

Influence and Impact: Social opinion leaders can leverage mindset principles to inspire positive change within their communities or organizations.

Advocacy and Leadership: Insights into resilience and adaptability empower social opinion leaders to navigate challenges and advocate for meaningful societal changes.

Personal Growth: The book provides guidance for continuous personal growth and self-improvement, supporting social opinion leaders in their roles as influencers and change agents.

Overall, "Power of Mindset" serves as a versatile resource for individuals across various roles and professions, equipping them with tools to cultivate a growth-oriented mindset, overcome challenges, and achieve personal and professional success.

SCOPE FOR FURTHER RESEARCH

Long-term Effects: Investigate the sustained impact of cultivating a growth mindset on individuals over extended periods, including effects on career trajectories, personal well-being, and relationships.

Cultural Variations: Explore how mindset theories apply across different cultural contexts and societies, examining factors that influence mindset development and outcomes.

Intervention Strategies: Develop and evaluate new interventions or educational programs aimed at promoting growth mindset in diverse settings such as schools, workplaces, and communities.

Neuroscientific Insights: Utilize neuroscientific methods to study the neural mechanisms underlying mindset formation and its behavioral implications.

Intersectionality: Investigate how factors like gender, socioeconomic status, and educational background intersect with mindset development and its effects on achievement and resilience.

Mindset and Leadership: Explore the role of mindset in effective leadership, including its influence on decision-making, organizational culture, and team performance.

Limitations:

Generalizability: The applicability of mindset theories may vary based on individual differences, cultural contexts, and socio-economic factors, limiting universal conclusions.

Measurement Challenges: Existing tools for assessing mindset may lack reliability or sensitivity in capturing nuanced changes in mindset over time or in diverse populations.

Longitudinal Studies: Many studies focus on short-term outcomes, necessitating more longitudinal research to understand lasting effects and developmental trajectories of mindset.

Causal Relationships: Establishing causal relationships between mindset and outcomes can be challenging due to confounding variables and the complexity of human behavior.

Ethical Considerations: Research involving mindset interventions must address ethical concerns related to informed consent, privacy, and potential unintended consequences.

Integration with Other Theories: While mindset theory is valuable, future research could explore its integration with other psychological theories to provide a more comprehensive understanding of human behavior.

Addressing these research areas and acknowledging these limitations can advance the field of mindset psychology, contributing to practical applications in education, leadership, and personal development.

May I Request You for a Review?

Could I kindly ask for your consideration to leave a review on the publisher's platform for the book? I hope you've found the book engaging and insightful on this captivating subject. While reviews might carry less weight for established authors, they hold immense value for writers like me who are emerging and lack a significant following. Your review could be instrumental in drawing more readers to my work, inspiring them to explore my books.

As you immerse yourself in the content of this book, I believe you'll be inclined to share your thoughts in a review. Writing your sentiments about the book will require just a brief two minutes of your time. Your support and engagement mean a lot to me, and I'm eager to see your review on the publisher's page. Your reviews contribute to the dialogue and feedback from readers, fostering a greater connection between authors and their audience.

I assure you, taking just a couple of minutes to share your thoughts on the book would be greatly appreciated. Your words hold the power to inspire and propel my passion for writing even further.

Thank you from the bottom of my heart for supporting my work. I eagerly await your review on the publisher page, where your words will resonate and touch the hearts of fellow readers.

Happy reading and heartfelt gratitude.

DISCLAIMER

The information presented in this book regarding the power of pure intention is based on our personal understanding, knowledge, and beliefs, supported by insights gained from various authorities and personal experiences. While some information is sourced from reliable references, it is not intended to substitute professional medical advice for specific conditions. Readers are advised to consult qualified experts before making decisions based on the content herein.

The author and publisher do not assume responsibility for any errors or omissions in the information provided in this book. Readers are encouraged to exercise their own judgment and seek professional advice as needed.

This disclaimer covers any potential harm, damage, or actions resulting from the implementation of suggestions contained in this book, which addresses complex life issues. By reading this book, you agree to understand and accept all associated risks. The content is for informational purposes only, and your use of this book indicates your acknowledgment and acceptance of this disclaimer.

While the suggestions presented in this book are generally applicable and beneficial across various fields of activity, we cannot guarantee the specific outcomes or levels of success individual readers may achieve.

APPENDICES

Strategies to cultivate resilient and enduring mindset

Cultivating a resilient and enduring mindset involves developing the ability to bounce back from setbacks, adapt to challenges, and maintain a positive outlook in the face of adversity. Here are strategies to help cultivate a resilient and enduring mindset:

Develop Self-Awareness: Understand your strengths, weaknesses, and emotional triggers. Self-awareness allows you to recognize when you're facing challenges and proactively manage your reactions.

Set Realistic Goals: Establish clear, achievable goals that align with your values and aspirations. Break larger goals into smaller, manageable tasks to maintain motivation and track progress.

Practice Positive Self-Talk: Replace negative thoughts with affirming and constructive self-talk. Encourage yourself during difficult times and focus on solutions rather than dwelling on problems.

Build a Support Network: Cultivate relationships with supportive friends, family members, mentors, or colleagues.

Lean on your support network for encouragement, advice, and perspective during challenging periods.

Embrace Change and Adaptability: Develop flexibility in responding to changing circumstances or unexpected events. Embrace change as an opportunity for growth and learning, rather than resisting it.

Learn from Setbacks: View setbacks and failures as valuable learning experiences. Analyze what went wrong, identify lessons learned, and use this knowledge to improve your approach in the future.

Maintain Perspective: Keep challenges in perspective by focusing on the bigger picture and long-term goals. Recognize that setbacks are temporary and part of the journey towards achieving success.

Practice Gratitude: Cultivate a habit of gratitude by acknowledging and appreciating the positive aspects of your life, even during difficult times. Gratitude helps maintain a positive outlook and resilience.

Take Care of Yourself: Prioritize self-care by maintaining a healthy lifestyle, including regular exercise, adequate sleep, and nutritious meals. Physical and mental well-being contribute to resilience.

Develop Problem-Solving Skills: Enhance your ability to solve problems effectively by breaking down complex issues into manageable steps. Seek creative solutions and remain proactive in addressing challenges.

Stay Persistent: Maintain perseverance and determination in pursuing your goals, even when faced with obstacles or setbacks. Stay committed to your values and vision for long-term success.

Celebrate Achievements: Acknowledge and celebrate your accomplishments, no matter how small. Recognizing progress boosts confidence and reinforces your resilience.

By incorporating these strategies into your mindset and daily practices, you can cultivate a resilient and enduring mindset that empowers you to navigate challenges, adapt to change, and achieve long-term success in various aspects of your life.

Strategies to cultivate positive thinking mindset

Cultivating a positive thinking mindset involves fostering optimism, resilience, and a constructive outlook on life's challenges and opportunities. Here are strategies to help cultivate a positive thinking mindset:

Practice Gratitude Daily: Start each day by acknowledging and appreciating the positive aspects of your life. Keep a gratitude journal to record things you are thankful for, fostering a positive perspective.

Challenge Negative Thoughts: Recognize negative thought patterns and replace them with positive affirmations and constructive self-talk. Focus on solutions and possibilities rather than dwelling on problems.

Surround Yourself with Positivity: Spend time with supportive and uplifting individuals who inspire and encourage you. Engage in activities and conversations that promote optimism and positivity.

Visualize Success: Use visualization techniques to imagine achieving your goals and experiencing positive outcomes. Visualizing success can increase motivation and reinforce your belief in your abilities.

Set Realistic Goals: Establish clear, achievable goals that align with your values and aspirations. Break larger goals into smaller, manageable tasks to maintain momentum and celebrate progress.

Focus on Solutions: Approach challenges with a proactive mindset, focusing on finding solutions and learning opportunities. Use setbacks as chances for growth and improvement.

Practice Self-Compassion: Treat yourself with kindness and understanding, especially during difficult times. Accept imperfections and mistakes as part of the learning process without being overly critical.

Stay Present-Minded: Practice mindfulness to stay grounded in the present moment and reduce anxiety about the future. Mindfulness techniques, such as deep breathing or meditation, promote a calm and positive outlook.

Learn from Adversity: Embrace challenges as opportunities for personal growth and resilience. Reflect on past experiences to identify lessons learned and strengths gained.

Celebrate Small Wins: Acknowledge and celebrate your achievements, no matter how small. Recognizing progress boosts confidence and reinforces a positive mindset.

Limit Exposure to Negativity: Minimize exposure to negative news, gossip, or environments that drain your energy and optimism. Surround yourself with positivity and uplifting content instead.

Focus on Personal Growth: Invest in your personal development through learning, hobbies, or skills that bring you joy and fulfillment. Continuous growth fosters a sense of purpose and positivity.

By integrating these strategies into your daily life and mindset, you can cultivate a positive thinking mindset that promotes resilience, optimism, and a constructive approach to achieving your goals and overcoming challenges.

Strategies to cultivate personal growth mindset

Cultivating a personal growth mindset involves fostering a belief in your ability to learn, adapt, and improve through dedication and effort. Here are strategies to help cultivate a personal growth mindset:

Embrace Challenges: View challenges and obstacles as opportunities for growth and learning rather than setbacks. Approach new experiences with curiosity and a willingness to learn.

Set Learning Goals: Establish specific goals that focus on acquiring new skills, knowledge, or experiences. Break down larger goals into smaller, actionable steps to facilitate continuous progress.

Seek Feedback and Learn from Criticism: Solicit feedback from others to gain different perspectives and insights. Embrace constructive criticism as a means to identify areas for improvement and personal development.

Develop Resilience: Build resilience by maintaining a positive attitude in the face of setbacks or failures. See setbacks as temporary and use them as opportunities to refine your approach and grow stronger.

Cultivate Curiosity: Stay curious about the world around you and actively seek out opportunities to expand your knowledge and understanding. Ask questions and explore different viewpoints.

Learn from Mistakes: Reflect on past experiences, including failures or mistakes, to extract valuable lessons. Use these lessons to adjust your approach and improve outcomes in the future.

Embrace Continuous Learning: Commit to lifelong learning by pursuing education, training, or self-improvement initiatives. Stay informed about industry trends, advancements, and best practices.

Practice Self-Reflection: Set aside time for self-reflection to assess your progress, strengths, and areas for growth. Identify patterns of behavior or thought that may be hindering your personal development.

Stay Flexible and Adaptive: Remain open to change and adaptable in response to evolving circumstances or opportunities. Embrace uncertainty as a chance to explore new possibilities and innovate.

Celebrate Progress: Acknowledge and celebrate your achievements, no matter how small. Recognizing milestones and successes boosts confidence and reinforces a commitment to personal growth.

Build a Supportive Network: Surround yourself with supportive individuals who encourage and challenge you to pursue personal growth. Seek mentorship or join communities that share similar goals.

Stay Committed to Goals: Maintain persistence and determination in pursuing your personal growth objectives. Stay focused on your long-term vision while adjusting strategies as needed to stay on track.

By integrating these strategies into your mindset and daily practices, you can cultivate a personal growth mindset that empowers you to continuously learn, adapt, and achieve your full potential in various aspects of life and work.

Strategies to cultivate environmental mastery mindset

Cultivating an environmental mastery mindset involves developing a sense of control, competence, and effectiveness in managing your surroundings and circumstances. Here are strategies to help cultivate an environmental mastery mindset:

Set Clear Goals and Priorities: Define specific goals and priorities that align with your values and aspirations. Establish a roadmap for achieving these goals to create a sense of direction and purpose.

Develop Problem-Solving Skills: Enhance your ability to identify challenges and find effective solutions. Break down complex problems into manageable tasks and take proactive steps to address them.

Build Organizational Skills: Cultivate habits and routines that enhance your organizational skills. Use tools such as calendars, task lists, and productivity apps to manage time effectively and stay on track with commitments.

Seek Knowledge and Information: Stay informed about relevant topics, trends, and developments in your environment. Continuously seek opportunities for learning and skill development to stay ahead.

Manage Stress and Emotions: Develop strategies to cope with stress and regulate your emotions effectively. Practice mindfulness, deep breathing, or relaxation techniques to maintain composure in challenging situations.

Take Initiative and Responsibility: Take ownership of your actions and decisions. Demonstrate initiative by identifying opportunities for improvement or innovation within your environment and taking decisive action.

Cultivate Adaptability: Embrace change and remain flexible in response to shifting circumstances or unexpected events. Adapt your strategies and approaches as needed to navigate challenges effectively.

Build a Support Network: Surround yourself with supportive individuals who provide encouragement, advice, and constructive feedback. Seek mentorship or join professional networks to broaden your perspective.

Celebrate Achievements: Acknowledge and celebrate your successes, no matter how small. Recognizing milestones and accomplishments boosts confidence and reinforces your ability to influence your environment positively.

Promote Collaboration and Teamwork: Foster collaboration with others to achieve common goals and objectives. Value diverse perspectives and leverage collective strengths to address complex challenges.

Evaluate and Reflect: Regularly evaluate your progress and performance in managing your environment. Reflect on lessons learned from successes and setbacks to refine your strategies and improve outcomes.

Maintain a Positive Outlook: Cultivate optimism and resilience in facing challenges. Focus on solutions and opportunities for growth rather than being overwhelmed by obstacles.

By incorporating these strategies into your mindset and daily practices, you can cultivate an environmental mastery mindset that empowers you to navigate your surroundings effectively, achieve goals, and foster positive change in your personal and professional life.

Strategies to cultivate gratitude mindset

Cultivating a gratitude mindset involves fostering appreciation, positivity, and acknowledgment of the good things in your life, even amidst challenges. Here are strategies to help cultivate a gratitude mindset:

Keep a Gratitude Journal: Dedicate time each day or week to write down things you are grateful for. Reflect on both big and small blessings, such as relationships, opportunities, or moments of joy.

Start and End the Day with Gratitude: Begin your day by focusing on things you are thankful for, setting a positive tone. Similarly, before bed, reflect on the positive aspects of your day, reinforcing a grateful mindset.

Express Appreciation: Regularly express gratitude to others. Thank friends, family, colleagues, or even strangers for their kindness, support, or contributions. Verbalize or write notes of thanks to deepen connections.

Shift Focus from Wants to Appreciation: Instead of focusing solely on what you lack or desire, redirect your attention to what you already have and appreciate. This shift in perspective enhances contentment and satisfaction.

Practice Mindfulness: Cultivate mindfulness to stay present and fully engage in the moment. Notice and appreciate the beauty of your surroundings, the taste of food, or the warmth of relationships.

Turn Challenges into Opportunities: View challenges and setbacks as opportunities for growth and learning. Reflect on how difficulties have strengthened your resilience or taught you valuable lessons.

Volunteer or Help Others: Engage in acts of kindness or volunteer work. Contributing to others' well-being fosters gratitude by recognizing your ability to make a positive impact in the lives of others.

Celebrate Progress and Milestones: Acknowledge and celebrate your achievements, no matter how small. Recognizing milestones and personal growth reinforces a sense of accomplishment and gratitude.

Create Rituals of Appreciation: Establish rituals or routines that remind you to be grateful. This could include gratitude exercises, prayers, or moments of reflection throughout the day.

Limit Exposure to Negativity: Minimize exposure to negative news or influences that can overshadow gratitude. Choose to focus on positive content, conversations, and relationships that uplift and inspire.

Practice Self-Compassion: Treat yourself with kindness and understanding, especially during challenging times. Recognize your efforts and achievements, offering yourself the same gratitude you extend to others.

Reflect on Lessons Learned: Regularly reflect on experiences and how they've contributed to your growth and well-being. Appreciate the journey, recognizing the value of both joys and hardships.

By integrating these strategies into your daily life and mindset, you can cultivate a gratitude mindset that enhances positivity, resilience, and overall well-being. Embracing gratitude fosters a deeper appreciation for life's blessings and cultivates a more fulfilling and optimistic outlook.

Strategies to cultivate problem solving mindset

Cultivating a problem-solving mindset involves developing the ability to approach challenges systematically, creatively, and effectively. Here are strategies to help cultivate a problem-solving mindset:

Define the Problem Clearly: Begin by clearly defining the problem or challenge you are facing. Break down complex issues into smaller, manageable components to understand the root cause and scope of the problem.

Gather Relevant Information: Collect pertinent data, facts, and insights related to the problem. Conduct research, seek input from others, and gather diverse perspectives to gain a comprehensive understanding of the issue.

Generate Multiple Solutions: Brainstorm and explore various potential solutions without immediately judging or dismissing ideas. Encourage creativity and innovation by considering unconventional approaches or combinations.

Evaluate and Analyze Solutions: Assess each potential solution based on feasibility, effectiveness, and alignment with your goals. Consider potential risks, costs, and benefits associated with each option before making a decision.

Take Action: Implement the chosen solution or course of action decisively. Break down implementation steps into actionable tasks, set deadlines, and allocate resources as needed to move forward effectively.

Monitor Progress and Adjust: Continuously monitor the implementation of your solution. Evaluate progress, gather feedback, and make adjustments or refinements as necessary to optimize outcomes.

Learn from Mistakes and Setbacks: View setbacks or failures as learning opportunities. Analyze what went wrong, identify lessons learned, and apply insights to improve future problem-solving approaches.

Develop Critical Thinking Skills: Enhance your ability to analyze information, identify patterns, and make informed decisions. Practice critical thinking through exercises, puzzles, or debates to sharpen your problem-solving acumen.

Seek Feedback and Collaboration: Solicit feedback from peers, mentors, or subject matter experts to gain fresh perspectives and insights. Collaborate with others to leverage diverse skills and knowledge in solving complex problems.

Stay Persistent and Resilient: Maintain persistence and determination in tackling challenges. Remain resilient in the face of setbacks, remaining focused on finding viable solutions and achieving your objectives.

Use Tools and Resources: Utilize problem-solving tools and techniques, such as root cause analysis, SWOT analysis, or decision matrices, to structure your approach and enhance decision-making.

Celebrate Successes: Acknowledge and celebrate achievements throughout the problem-solving process. Recognize milestones, accomplishments, and the collective effort of your team to maintain motivation and morale.

By incorporating these strategies into your mindset and daily practices, you can cultivate a proactive and effective problem-solving mindset. This approach empowers you to tackle challenges with confidence, creativity, and resilience, ultimately driving continuous improvement and success in various aspects of your personal and professional life.

Strategies to cultivate honesty mindset

Cultivating an honesty mindset involves fostering integrity, transparency, and truthfulness in your thoughts, actions, and interactions with others. Here are strategies to help cultivate an honesty mindset:

Value Integrity: Commit to upholding high ethical standards and moral principles in all aspects of your life. Make integrity a cornerstone of your personal and professional conduct.

Be Truthful with Yourself: Practice self-reflection and introspection to understand your values, beliefs, and motivations. Be honest with yourself about your strengths, weaknesses, and areas for improvement.

Communicate Openly and Transparently: Foster open and transparent communication in your interactions with others. Share information honestly, clearly, and without hidden agendas.

Admit Mistakes and Learn from Them: Acknowledge and take responsibility for your mistakes or shortcomings. Use mistakes as opportunities for growth and learning rather than attempting to cover them up.

Practice Active Listening: Listen attentively to others without judgment or interruption. Seek to understand different perspectives and validate others' experiences through empathetic listening.

Avoid Gossip and Rumors: Refrain from spreading rumors, gossip, or misinformation about others. Respect confidentiality and uphold the privacy of individuals in your personal and professional circles.

Seek Feedback and Constructive Criticism: Solicit feedback from trusted sources to gain insights into how your actions and decisions are perceived. Welcome constructive criticism as an opportunity for self-improvement.

Set Ethical Standards: Establish clear ethical guidelines and principles that guide your decision-making and behavior. Hold yourself accountable to these standards in all situations.

Build Trustworthy Relationships: Cultivate trustworthy relationships based on honesty, reliability, and mutual respect. Demonstrate consistency and integrity in your interactions to earn and maintain trust.

Practice Empathy and Respect: Treat others with empathy, compassion, and respect. Consider how your words and actions impact others' feelings and well-being, fostering a culture of honesty and trust.

Stay True to Your Values: Align your actions with your core values and principles. Make decisions that reflect honesty and integrity, even when faced with difficult choices or temptations.

Reflect on Ethical Dilemmas: Regularly reflect on ethical dilemmas you encounter and consider the potential consequences of different courses of action. Choose paths that uphold honesty and ethical behavior.

By integrating these strategies into your mindset and daily practices, you can cultivate an honesty mindset that promotes trust, integrity, and ethical behavior in all aspects of your personal and professional life. Honesty not only builds credibility and respect but also fosters meaningful and authentic relationships with others.

Strategies to cultivate co-operative mindset

Cultivating a cooperative mindset involves fostering collaboration, teamwork, and a willingness to work together towards common goals. Here are strategies to help cultivate a cooperative mindset:

Value Collaboration: Embrace the value of working together with others to achieve shared objectives. Recognize that collaboration can leverage diverse strengths and perspectives for greater innovation and success.

Build Trust: Establish trust and mutual respect with colleagues, team members, and collaborators. Demonstrate reliability, integrity, and transparency in your interactions to foster a foundation of trust.

Communicate Effectively: Practice clear and open communication to ensure understanding and alignment among team members. Share information, ideas, and feedback openly to facilitate collaboration.

Promote Active Listening: Listen attentively to others' viewpoints, ideas, and concerns. Validate and acknowledge different perspectives to foster a collaborative environment based on mutual understanding.

Encourage Diversity: Embrace diversity of thought, background, and expertise within teams. Value different viewpoints and approaches as opportunities to enrich discussions and decision-making processes.

Share Responsibilities: Distribute tasks and responsibilities equitably among team members. Encourage each person to contribute their unique skills and insights to achieve collective goals.

Set Clear Goals and Roles: Define clear goals, objectives, and roles within teams or collaborative efforts. Ensure clarity on expectations and responsibilities to minimize misunderstandings and promote accountability.

Celebrate Team Successes: Acknowledge and celebrate achievements and milestones reached through collaborative efforts. Recognize individual contributions and the collective impact of teamwork.

Resolve Conflicts Constructively: Address conflicts or disagreements promptly and constructively. Encourage open dialogue, active listening, and compromise to find mutually beneficial solutions.

Promote a Supportive Environment: Create a supportive and inclusive environment where team members feel valued, respected, and encouraged to contribute their ideas and perspectives.

Facilitate Knowledge Sharing: Share information, best practices, and lessons learned among team members. Foster a culture of continuous learning and improvement through knowledge exchange.

Lead by Example: Demonstrate cooperative behavior and attitudes in your own actions and interactions. Serve as a role model for collaboration, teamwork, and mutual support within your organization or community.

By integrating these strategies into your mindset and daily practices, you can cultivate a cooperative mindset that promotes effective teamwork, mutual respect, and shared success. Cooperation not only enhances productivity and innovation but also fosters a positive and supportive work culture where individuals thrive and contribute to collective achievements.

Strategies to cultivate happiness mindset

Cultivating a happiness mindset involves adopting habits and practices that promote positivity, gratitude, and overall well-being. Here are strategies to help cultivate a happiness mindset:

Practice Gratitude Daily: Start each day by reflecting on things you are grateful for. Keep a gratitude journal to record moments of appreciation and joy throughout your day.

Focus on the Present: Practice mindfulness to stay present and fully engage in the current moment. Pay attention to your surroundings, sensations, and experiences without judgment.

Cultivate Positive Relationships: Nurture supportive and positive relationships with family, friends, and colleagues. Spend time with people who uplift and inspire you, fostering a sense of connection and belonging.

Engage in Acts of Kindness: Perform acts of kindness for others, whether small gestures or larger contributions. Helping others fosters feelings of compassion, empathy, and fulfillment.

Set and Pursue Meaningful Goals: Establish clear goals that align with your values and passions. Pursue activities and achievements that bring a sense of purpose and fulfillment to your life.

Practice Self-Care: Prioritize your physical, emotional, and mental well-being through self-care activities. Incorporate exercise, healthy eating, adequate sleep, and relaxation techniques into your routine.

Celebrate Small Wins: Acknowledge and celebrate your accomplishments, no matter how small. Recognizing progress boosts self-confidence and reinforces positive behaviors.

Limit Exposure to Negativity: Minimize exposure to negative news, gossip, or environments that drain your energy and happiness. Choose to focus on positive content, relationships, and activities.

Find Joy in Simple Pleasures: Appreciate the little moments of joy and beauty in everyday life. Take time to savor experiences such as nature walks, hobbies, or quality time with loved ones.

Practice Optimism and Positive Thinking: Challenge negative thoughts and cultivate an optimistic outlook on life. Focus on solutions, opportunities for growth, and the potential for positive outcomes.

Engage in Leisure and Fun Activities: Schedule time for activities that bring you joy and relaxation. Pursue hobbies, interests, or creative pursuits that provide a sense of fulfillment and enjoyment.

Seek Professional Help if Needed: If feelings of unhappiness persist or impact your daily life, consider seeking support from a therapist or counselor. They can provide guidance and strategies to improve mental well-being.

By incorporating these strategies into your daily life and mindset, you can cultivate a happiness mindset that enhances overall well-being, resilience, and fulfillment. Happiness is a journey that involves intentional practices and habits to nurture positivity and joy in various aspects of life.

Strategies to cultivate prosperity mindset

Cultivating a prosperity mindset involves developing a positive attitude towards wealth, success, and abundance. Here are strategies to help cultivate a prosperity mindset:

Set Clear Financial Goals: Define specific financial goals that align with your values and aspirations. Break down long-term goals into smaller, actionable steps to track progress and maintain motivation.

Visualize Success and Abundance: Use visualization techniques to imagine achieving your financial goals and experiencing abundance. Visualizing success can enhance motivation and reinforce belief in your ability to create prosperity.

Practice Gratitude for Financial Success: Cultivate gratitude for your current financial situation and any progress made towards your goals. Appreciate the resources, opportunities, and support that contribute to your prosperity.

Adopt a Growth Mindset: Embrace a mindset that values learning, growth, and continuous improvement in your financial knowledge and skills. Seek opportunities to expand your expertise and explore new avenues for prosperity.

Take Calculated Risks: Be willing to step outside your comfort zone and take calculated risks in pursuit of financial growth and opportunities. Assess potential risks and rewards, and make informed decisions to maximize outcomes.

Manage Finances Effectively: Develop strong financial habits such as budgeting, saving, and investing wisely. Stay informed about financial markets, trends, and strategies to optimize your financial decisions.

Network and Build Relationships: Cultivate relationships with individuals who share similar financial goals and values. Network with mentors, advisors, and peers who can provide support, guidance, and opportunities for collaboration.

Focus on Value Creation: Identify ways to create value through your skills, products, or services. Prioritize delivering exceptional quality and exceeding customer expectations to build a strong foundation for prosperity.

Stay Positive and Resilient: Maintain a positive outlook and resilience in the face of challenges or setbacks. View obstacles as opportunities for growth and learning, and persist in pursuing your financial goals.

Invest in Personal Development: Invest in yourself through education, training, or personal development initiatives that enhance your knowledge, skills, and mindset. Continuous growth contributes to long-term prosperity.

Celebrate Financial Milestones: Acknowledge and celebrate achievements and milestones in your financial journey. Recognize progress, no matter how small, and use these successes as motivation to continue moving forward.

Give Back and Share Abundance: Practice generosity and contribute to causes or organizations that align with your values. Sharing your prosperity with others fosters a sense of fulfillment and reinforces a positive cycle of abundance.

By integrating these strategies into your mindset and daily practices, you can cultivate a prosperity mindset that promotes financial well-being, success, and abundance. Embrace opportunities for growth, stay focused on your goals, and maintain a positive attitude towards creating and experiencing prosperity in various aspects of your life.

Strategies to cultivate peaceful mindset

Cultivating a peaceful mindset involves fostering inner calm, tranquility, and emotional balance. Here are strategies to help cultivate a peaceful mindset:

Practice Mindfulness: Engage in mindfulness meditation or practices that promote present-moment awareness. Pay attention to your thoughts, emotions, and sensations without judgment, cultivating inner peace.

Simplify Your Life: Declutter your physical space and simplify your commitments and schedule. Reduce distractions and focus on what truly matters to create a sense of calm and clarity.

Establish a Routine: Create a daily routine that includes activities that promote relaxation and well-being, such as exercise, reading, or spending time in nature. Consistency can help stabilize emotions and reduce stress.

Practice Deep Breathing: Incorporate deep breathing exercises or techniques such as diaphragmatic breathing to promote relaxation and reduce anxiety. Deep breathing can help calm the mind and body.

Limit Exposure to Stressors: Identify sources of stress in your life and take steps to minimize or manage them effectively. This may involve setting boundaries, delegating tasks, or seeking support from others.

Cultivate Gratitude: Foster a sense of gratitude by regularly reflecting on things you are thankful for. Gratitude promotes positivity and contentment, contributing to a peaceful mindset.

Engage in Physical Activity: Participate in regular exercise or physical activity that suits your fitness level and preferences. Physical movement can release tension, improve mood, and promote relaxation.

Practice Forgiveness: Let go of resentment or anger towards yourself and others. Practice forgiveness as a way to release negative emotions and cultivate inner peace and harmony.

Connect with Nature: Spend time outdoors in natural environments such as parks, forests, or near water bodies. Nature has a calming effect on the mind and body, reducing stress and promoting relaxation.

Engage in Creative Expression: Explore creative outlets such as art, music, writing, or crafts. Creative expression can be therapeutic, providing an outlet for emotions and promoting relaxation.

Set Boundaries: Establish clear boundaries in your relationships and commitments to protect your time, energy, and emotional well-being. Respect your limits and prioritize self-care.

Seek Support and Connection: Build and maintain supportive relationships with friends, family, or community members. Share your thoughts and feelings with trusted individuals who offer empathy and understanding.

By incorporating these strategies into your daily life and mindset, you can cultivate a peaceful mindset that enhances emotional well-being, reduces stress, and promotes inner tranquility. Embrace practices that resonate with you personally and create a harmonious environment conducive to peace and serenity.

Action steps to achieve the same

To achieve a peaceful mindset, you can take practical action steps that promote inner calm and emotional balance. Here are actionable steps you can implement:

Morning Routine for Peace: Start your day with a calming morning routine. This might include meditation, deep breathing exercises, or a moment of gratitude to set a peaceful tone for the day.

Create a Peaceful Environment: Designate a space in your home or workplace that promotes relaxation. Add elements like plants, soothing colors, or calming music to create a peaceful atmosphere.

Practice Mindful Breathing: Throughout the day, practice mindful breathing exercises. Take slow, deep breaths, focusing on the sensation of air entering and leaving your body to reduce stress and increase relaxation.

Schedule Regular Breaks: Incorporate breaks into your daily schedule to rest and recharge. Use breaks for stretching, walking, or simply taking a few minutes to clear your mind and relax.

Limit Media Consumption: Reduce exposure to negative news or social media that can contribute to stress and anxiety. Choose positive and uplifting content that supports your peace of mind.

Practice Gratitude Journaling: Keep a gratitude journal and write down three things you are grateful for each day. Reflecting on positive aspects of your life can shift your focus towards peace and contentment.

Set Realistic Goals: Break down larger goals into smaller, achievable tasks. Prioritize tasks that align with your values and contribute to your overall well-being, reducing feelings of overwhelm and promoting peace.

Practice Progressive Muscle Relaxation: Learn and practice progressive muscle relaxation techniques. Tense and then relax different muscle groups in your body to release physical tension and promote relaxation.

Engage in Physical Activity: Incorporate regular exercise into your routine. Physical activity releases endorphins, reduces stress hormones, and promotes a sense of well-being and calm.

Practice Active Listening: Improve your relationships and reduce conflict by practicing active listening. Give your full attention to others without judgment or interruption, fostering understanding and harmony.

Establish Boundaries: Set boundaries in your personal and professional life to protect your time and energy. Learn to say no to commitments or situations that compromise your peace of mind.

Seek Support and Connection: Connect with supportive friends, family members, or a counselor. Share your thoughts and feelings openly, and seek guidance or perspective when needed to maintain emotional balance.

By consistently implementing these action steps, given as examples, you can alter and add more to cultivate a peaceful mindset that promotes inner calm, emotional resilience, and overall well-being. Adjust these steps to fit your lifestyle and preferences, ensuring they contribute positively to your journey towards peace and tranquility.

REFERENCES FOR FURTHER LEARNING

Few resources and suggestions for deeper study and understanding of mindset and personal development:

Books:

"Mindset: The New Psychology of Success" by Carol S. Dweck - Provides foundational insights into fixed vs. growth mindsets and their implications.

"Grit: The Power of Passion and Perseverance" by Angela Duckworth - Explores the role of perseverance and resilience in achieving long-term goals.

"Drive: The Surprising Truth About What Motivates Us" by Daniel H. Pink - Discusses motivation and the importance of intrinsic factors like autonomy, mastery, and purpose.

"The Power of Habit: Why We Do What We Do in Life and Business" by Charles Duhigg - Offers insights into how habits shape behavior and ways to change them effectively.

"Atomic Habits: An Easy & Proven Way to Build Good Habits & Break Bad Ones" by James Clear - Practical strategies for habit formation and personal development.

Titles by Brené Brown - Known for her work on vulnerability, courage, and resilience.

"Thinking, Fast and Slow" by Daniel Kahneman - Explores cognitive biases and decision-making processes.

"The Talent Code: Greatness Isn't Born. It's Grown. Here's How" by Daniel Coyle - Focuses on skill development and talent.

"Mindfulness in Plain English" by Bhante Henepola Gunaratana - Offers practical insights into mindfulness practice.

"The 7 Habits of Highly Effective People" by Stephen R. Covey - Classic on personal effectiveness and growth.

"Outliers: The Story of Success" by Malcolm Gladwell - Explores factors contributing to high achievement.

"The Happiness Advantage: How a Positive Brain Fuels Success in Work and Life" by Shawn Achor - Discusses the connection between happiness and success.

"Start with Why: How Great Leaders Inspire Everyone to Take Action" by Simon Sinek - Focuses on purpose-driven leadership and motivation.

"Peak: Secrets from the New Science of Expertise" by Anders Ericsson and Robert Pool - Discusses deliberate practice and expertise.

"The Art of Learning: An Inner Journey to Optimal Performance" by Josh Waitzkin - Insights on learning, adaptation, and mastery.

Websites and Articles:

Mindset Works - Provides resources, research articles, and tools for educators and individuals interested in growth mindset development. (Website: mindsetworks.com)

Positive Psychology Program - Offers articles, courses, and tools related to positive psychology, resilience, and personal growth. (Website: positivepsychology.com)

Greater Good Science Center - Resources on the science of well-being, including articles on resilience, mindfulness, and social-emotional learning. (Website: greatergood.berkeley.edu)

Psychology Today - Features a wide range of articles on mindset, personal development, and psychology. (Website: psychologytoday.com)

Harvard Business Review - Articles on leadership, organizational psychology, and personal effectiveness. (Website: hbr.org)

Personal Growth & Development section on Medium - Offers articles on mindset, productivity, and personal growth.

Center for Compassion and Altruism Research and Education (CCARE) - Resources on compassion and resilience.

Mindful.org - Articles and practices on mindfulness and well-being.

Harvard Health Publishing - Offers insights into mental health, well-being, and resilience.

Stanford Center for Compassion and Altruism Research and Education (CCARE) - Research and resources on compassion and personal growth.

Chopra.com - Articles and resources on holistic well-being, including mindfulness and meditation.

Forbes Leadership section - Features articles on leadership, personal development, and resilience.

The Positive Psychology People - Blog and articles on positive psychology and personal growth.

The Art of Manliness - Offers practical advice and insights on personal development and self-improvement.

Business Insider Strategy section - Articles on leadership, career development, and personal growth strategies.

Podcasts and TED Talks:

TED Talks: Ideas Worth Spreading - Various talks on mindset, resilience, motivation, and personal growth. (Website: ted.com/talks)

The Tim Ferriss Show - Podcast featuring interviews with experts on productivity, mindset, and personal development. (Website: tim.blog/podcast/)

The School of Greatness by Lewis Howes - Podcast exploring stories from influential individuals and their insights on success and personal growth. (Website: lewishowes.com/blog/)

These resources offer a blend of theoretical insights, practical strategies, and inspirational stories to support ongoing learning and development in mindset and personal growth.

ABOUT THE AUTHOR

Samapti Banerjee, goes by SAM, is a seasoned author and thought leader dedicated to empowering individuals through transformative insights and practical strategies. With a background in Engineering and Project Management and a passion for helping people for personal development, Sam explores the profound impact of mindset on success and fulfillment.

Having authored acclaimed works such as "The Idea Catalyst: Igniting Your Creative Potential for Success" and "The Breakthrough Code", co-authored with Dr. Gurudas Bandyopadhyay, Sam has established a reputation for guiding readers towards unlocking their full potential. Through these books, she integrates psychology, creativity, and leadership principles to inspire readers to embrace innovation and resilience in their personal and professional lives.

"Power of Mindset" represents Sam's latest endeavor, offering readers a comprehensive guide to cultivating a growth-oriented mindset. With a focus on overcoming self-limiting beliefs and harnessing resilience, this book equips readers with actionable steps to achieve their goals and navigate challenges with confidence.

Sam continues to advocate for lifelong learning and growth, emphasizing the importance of mindset in shaping one's reality. Through a blend of research-backed insights and practical wisdom, Samapti empowers readers to embrace change, cultivate resilience, and achieve lasting success.

Dr. Gurudas Bandyopadhyay is a serial author with a profound understanding of human psychology and personal development. Published 27 books in different genres. He has established himself as a leading voice in the field of empowerment and transformative thinking. Driven by a passion for helping individuals unlock their potential, his works resonate with readers worldwide, offering deep insights and practical guidance for achieving personal growth and inner fulfillment. Drawing from his extensive experience in psychology and holistic wellness, Dr. Bandyopadhyay's writings inspire readers to cultivate a positive mindset and embrace the power of their thoughts for a more enriched and purposeful life.

To connect with the author

Visit Author Website https://drgurudas.com

More Books From the Author

Visit author website https://drgurudas.com

★★★

The Upcoming Book

Self-Care SOLUTION: Elevate Energy, Conquer Anxiety, Achieve Balance, and Flourish in Every Area of Life."

Discover the transformative power of self-care with "Self-Care SOLUTION". This comprehensive guide is your roadmap to cultivating holistic well-being and achieving harmony in every aspect of your life.

This transformative guidebook aims to help people achieve holistic well-being through structured self-care practices. From physical health to emotional resilience, social connections, and financial stability; the book offers practical strategies and actionable insights. Readers will learn to cultivate a growth-oriented mindset, manage stress effectively, nurture meaningful relationships, and align with their life's purpose. With a focus on balance and fulfillment, this book empowers readers to elevate their energy, conquer anxiety, and flourish in every aspect of their lives.

www.ingramcontent.com/pod-product-compliance
Lightning Source LLC
Chambersburg PA
CBHW071911210526
45479CB00002B/367